50 Chickens Coloring Book for Adults

50 Stress Relieving Chicken and Rooster Coloring Pages of Charming Grayscale Illustrations for Adults, Teens and Older Kids

I0491921

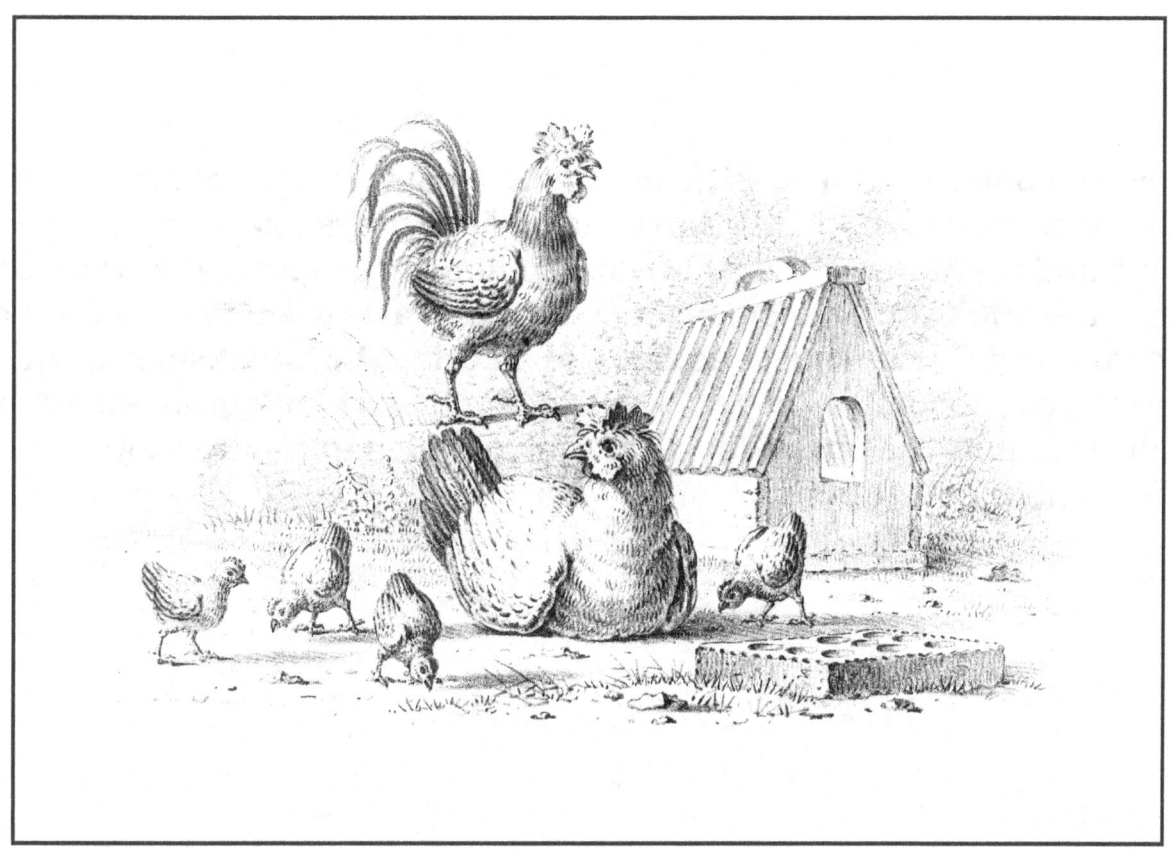

Ada Ashley

©LeVintagePrintage

In this coloring book, you will find 50 charming illustrations from famous illustra-
tors of the past, reproduced true to original in light grayscale, perfect for realis-
tic coloring and art therapy relaxation. Illustrations are reproduced without hard
outlines for the opportunity to color them as actual artwork and be proud to cut
out and display after finishing. In addition to coloring, this book allows you to
practice drawing, shading, and tracing based on the artwork of master illustra-
tors. Coloring sheets are one-sided and blank on the back so they can be cut out
for display or separate coloring.

Ada Ashley

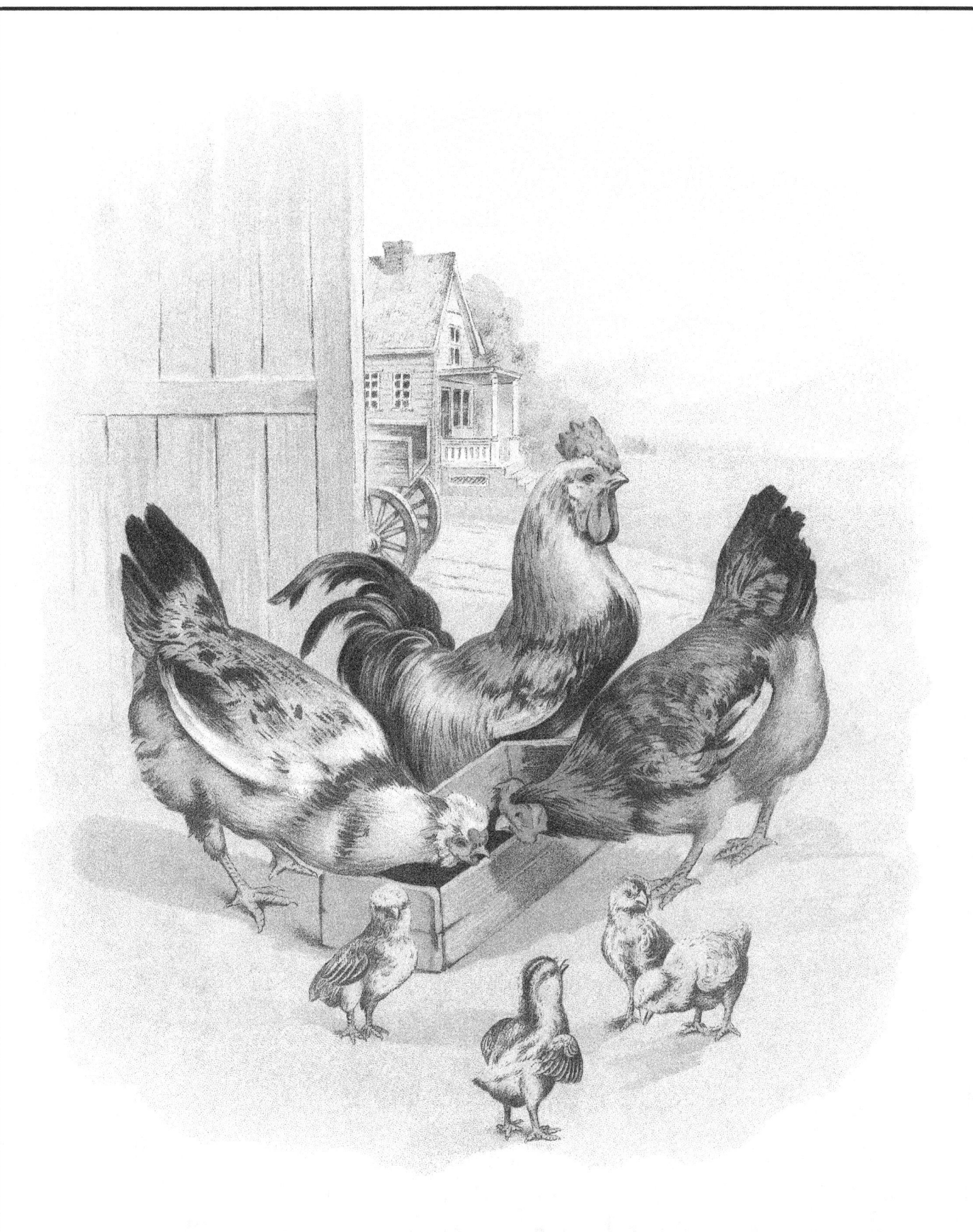

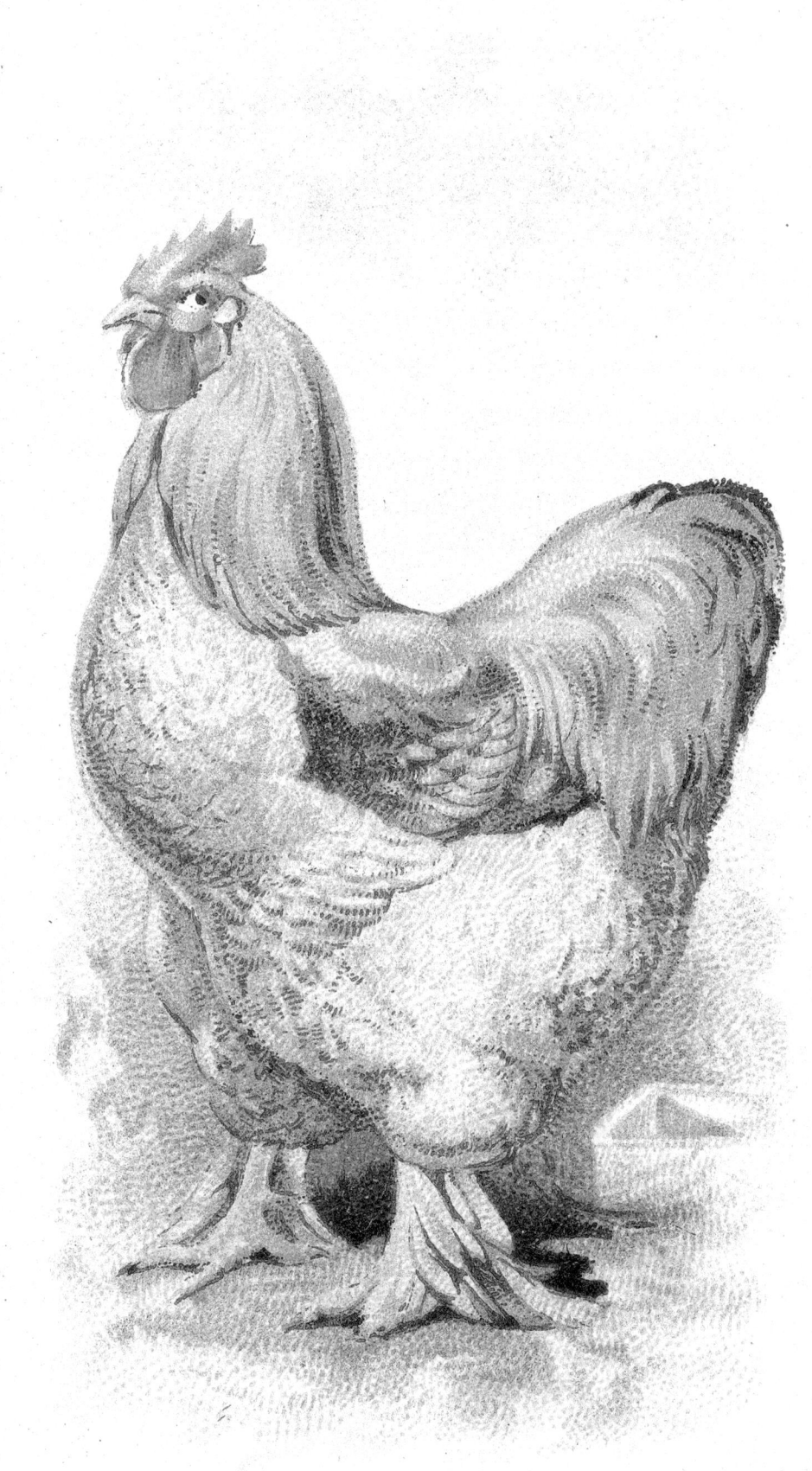

BUFF COCHIN CHINA COCK.

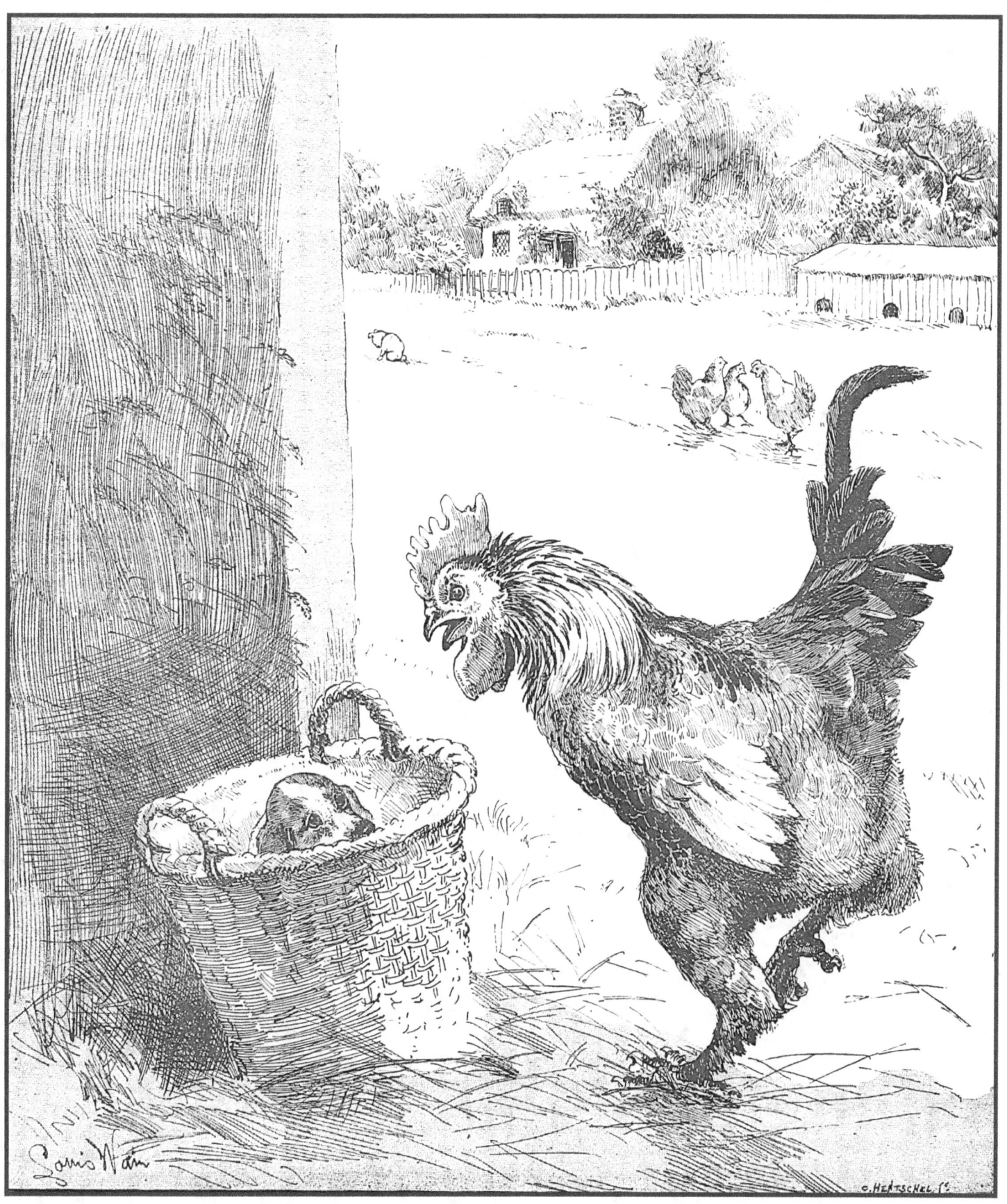

BLACK-BREASTED RED GAME COCK.

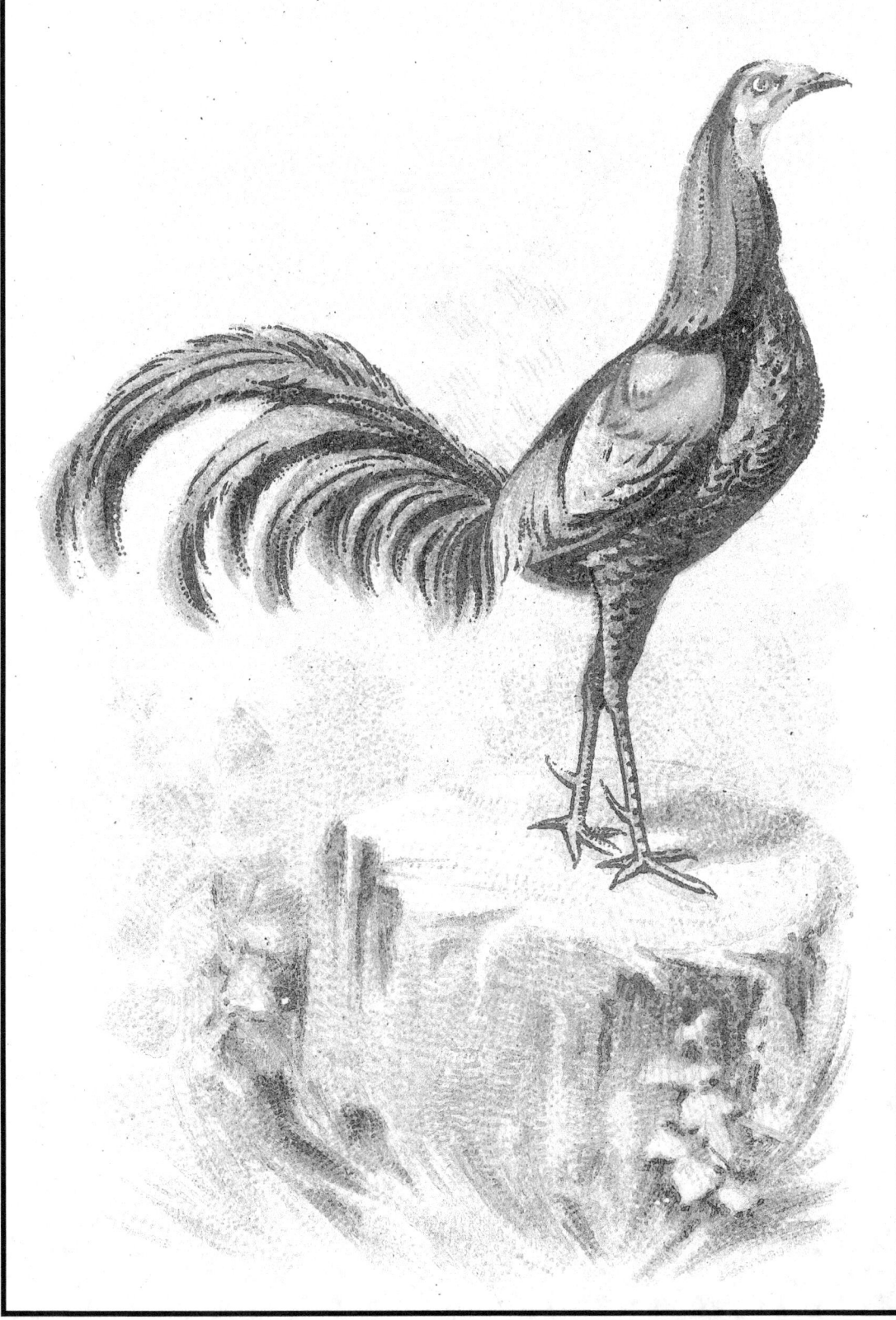

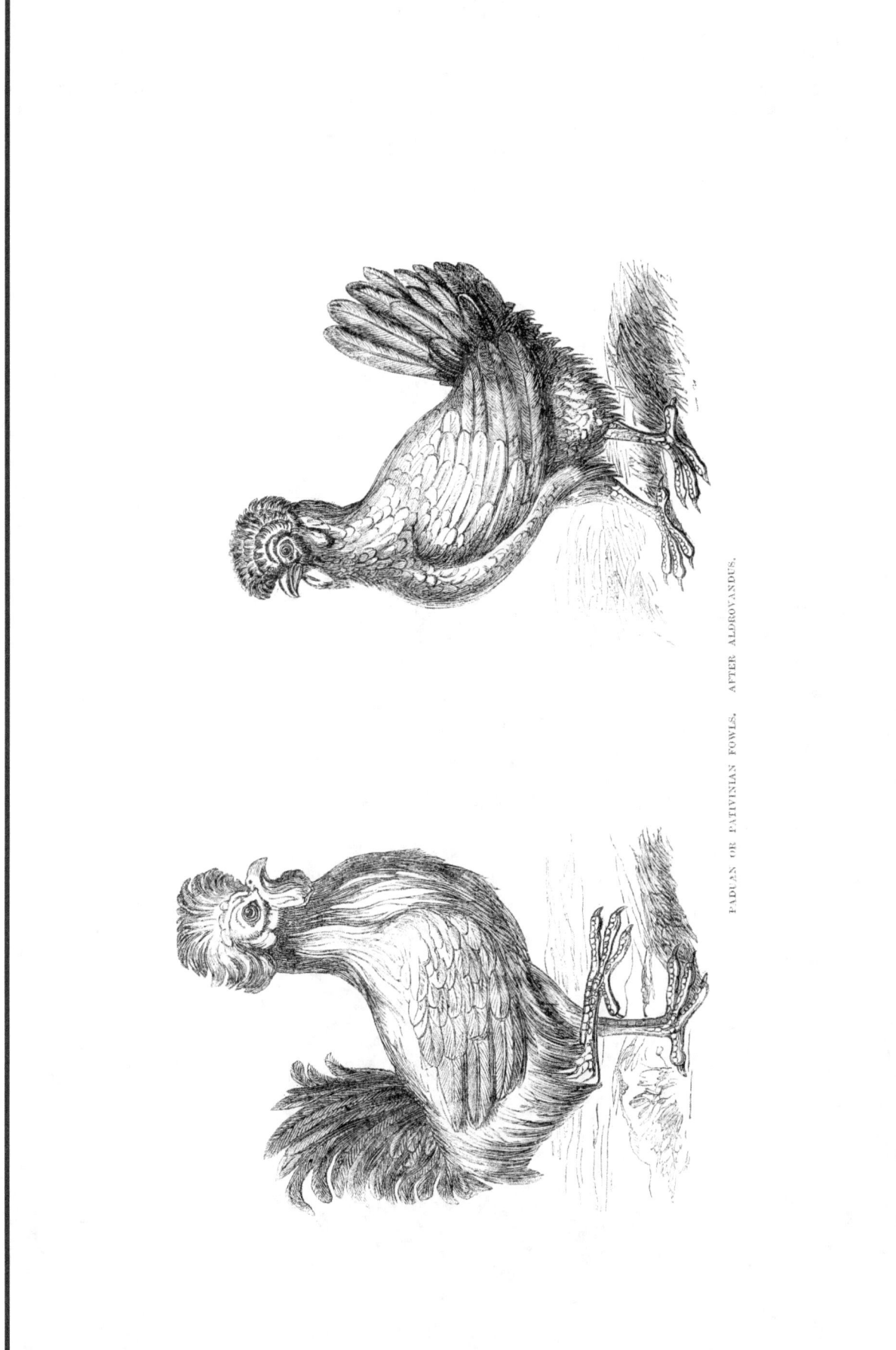

PADUAN OR PATAVINIAN FOWLS. AFTER ALDROVANDUS.

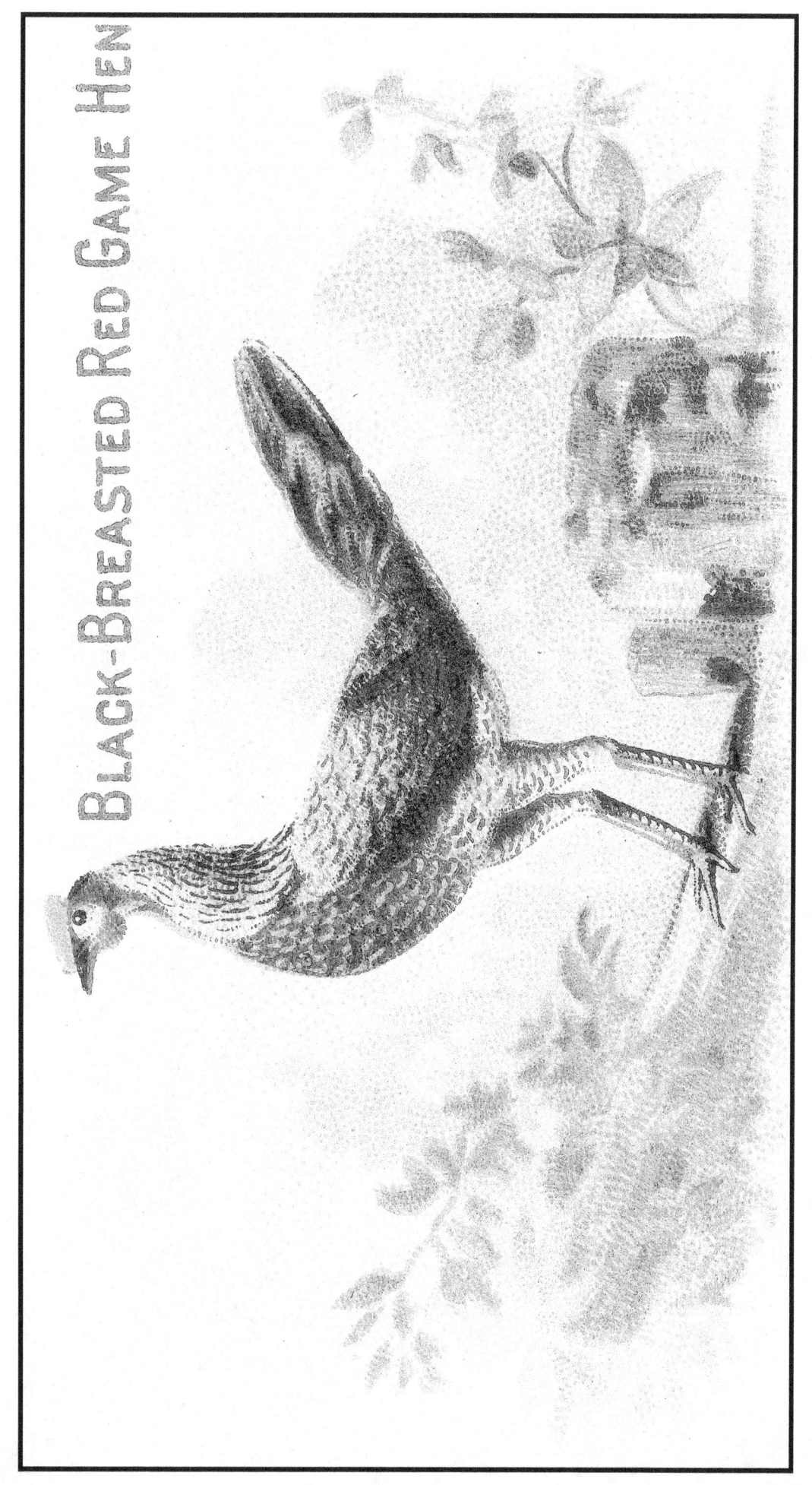

BLACK-BREASTED RED GAME HEN

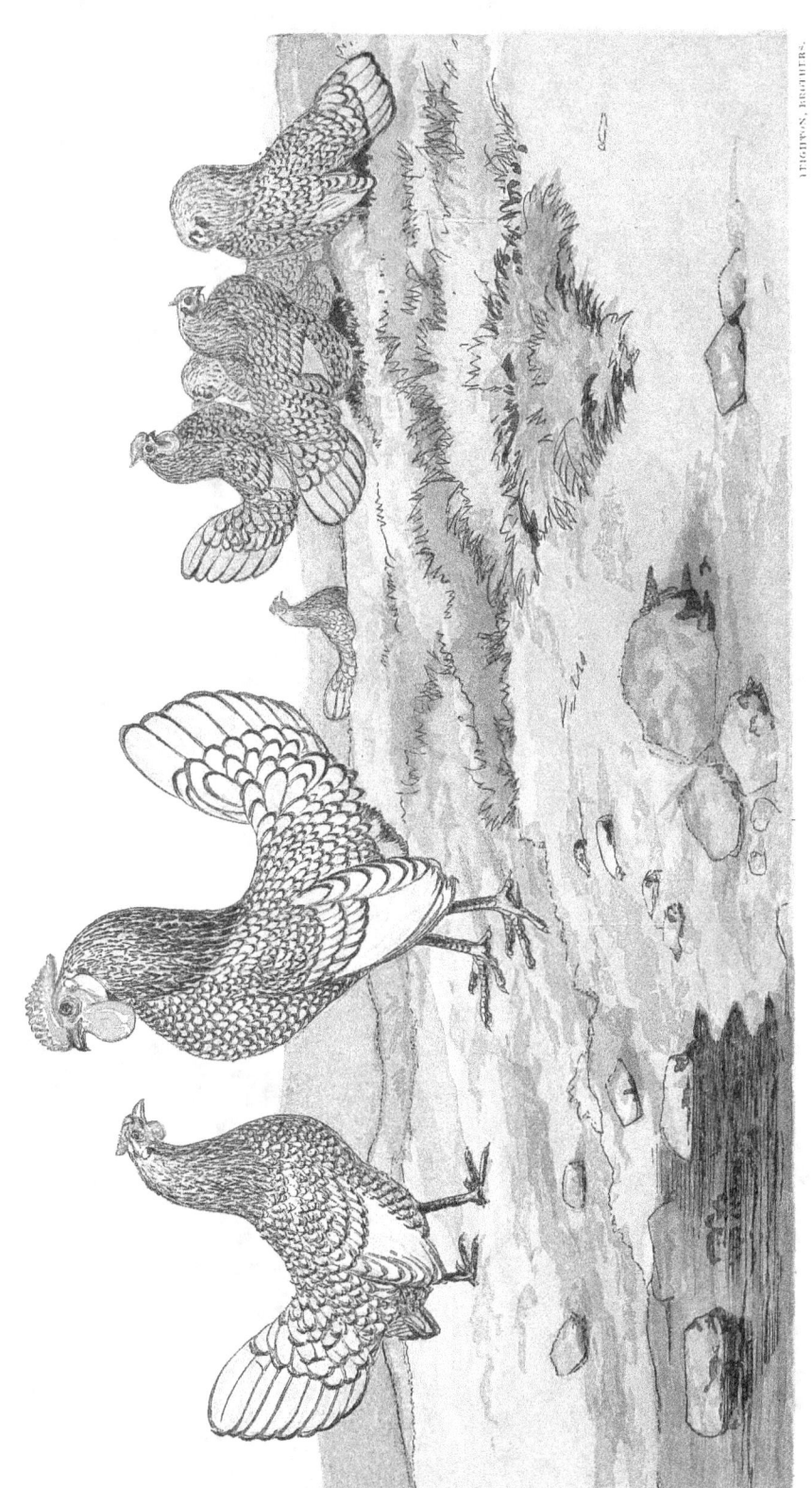

GOLD AND SILVER LACED BANTAMS.

LEIGHTON, BROTHERS.

SILVER-PENCILED WYANDOTTES

LIGHT BRAHMAS

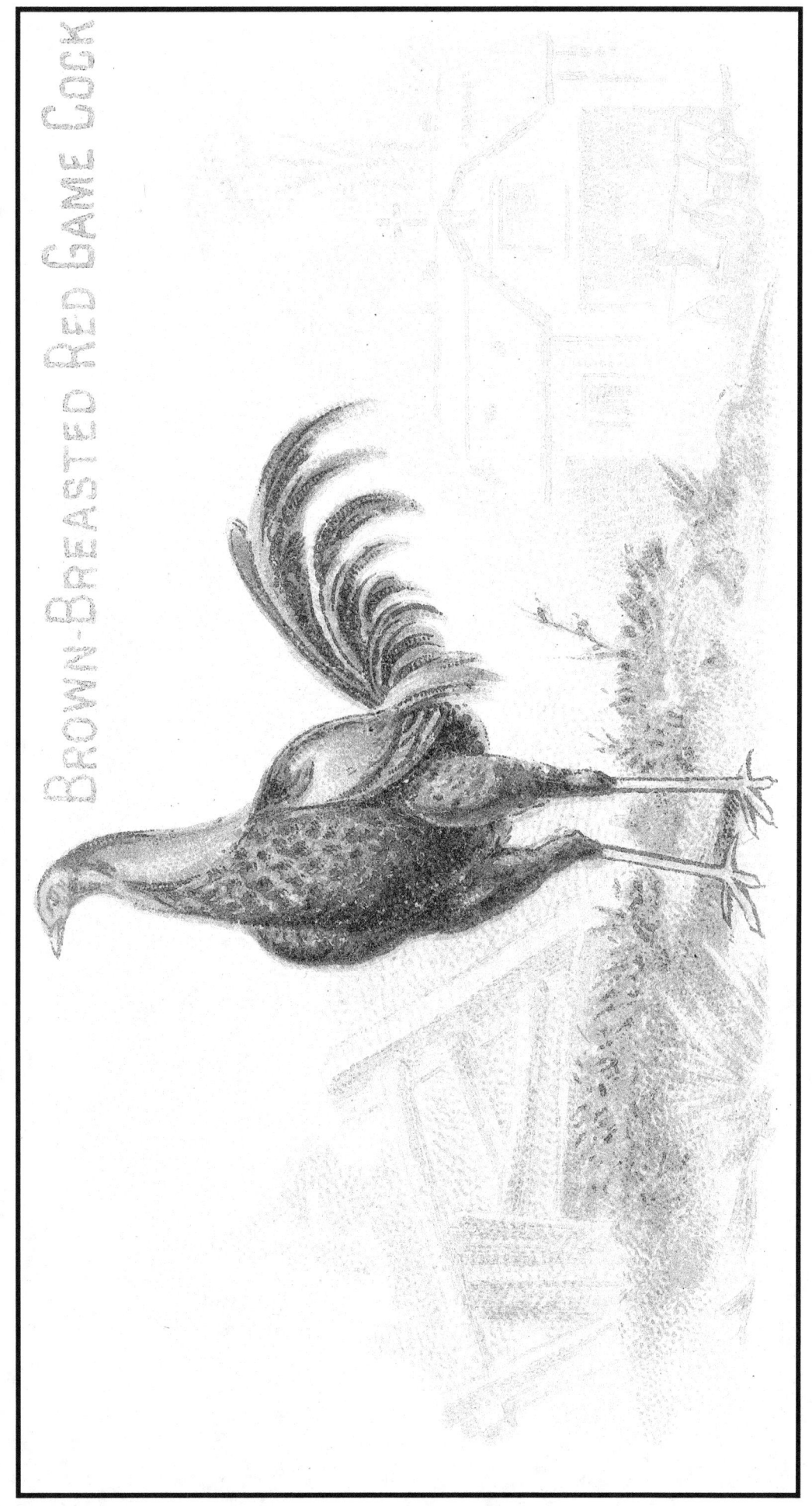

BROWN-BREASTED RED GAME COCK

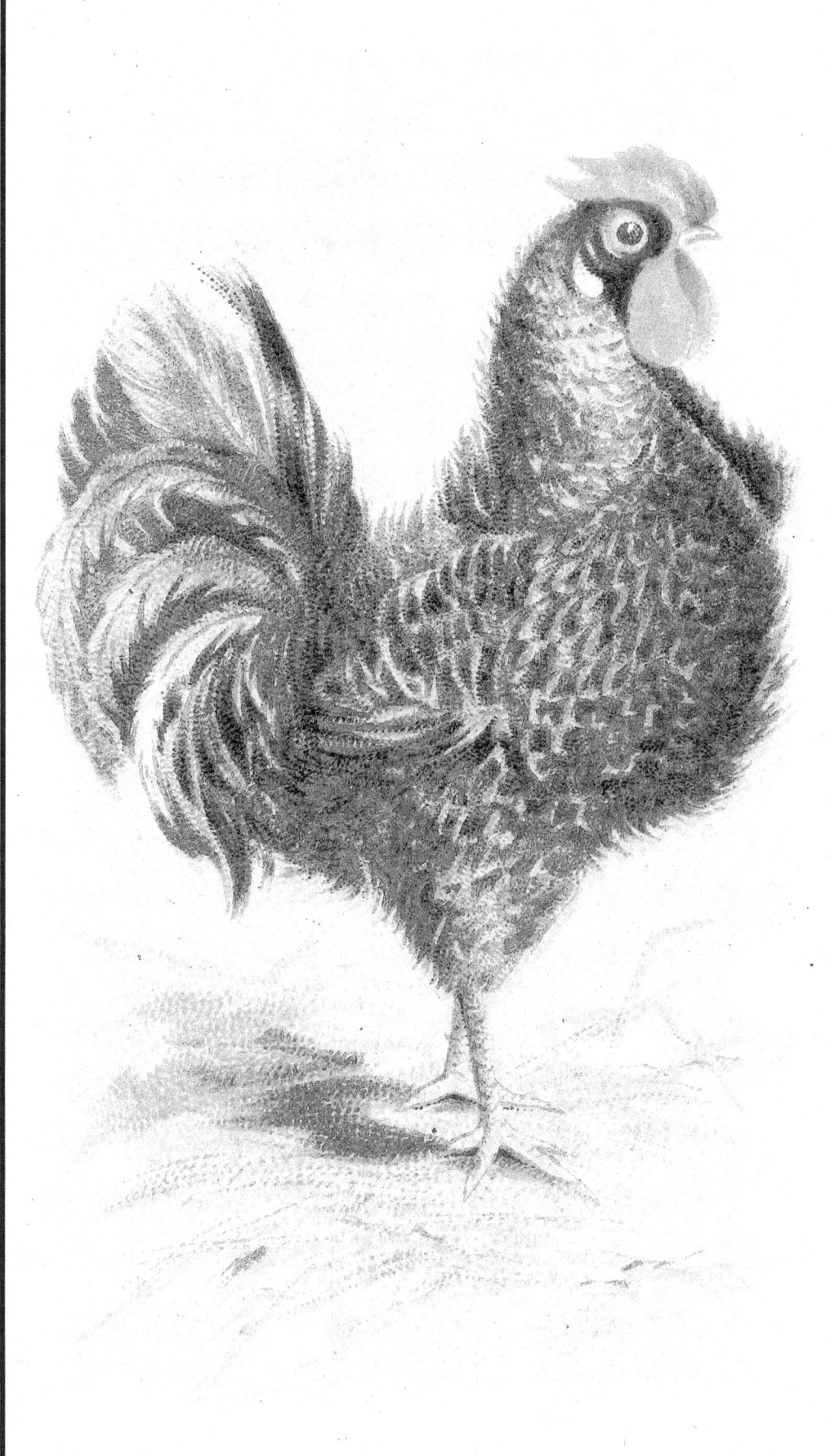

BLACK FRIZZLED FOWL.

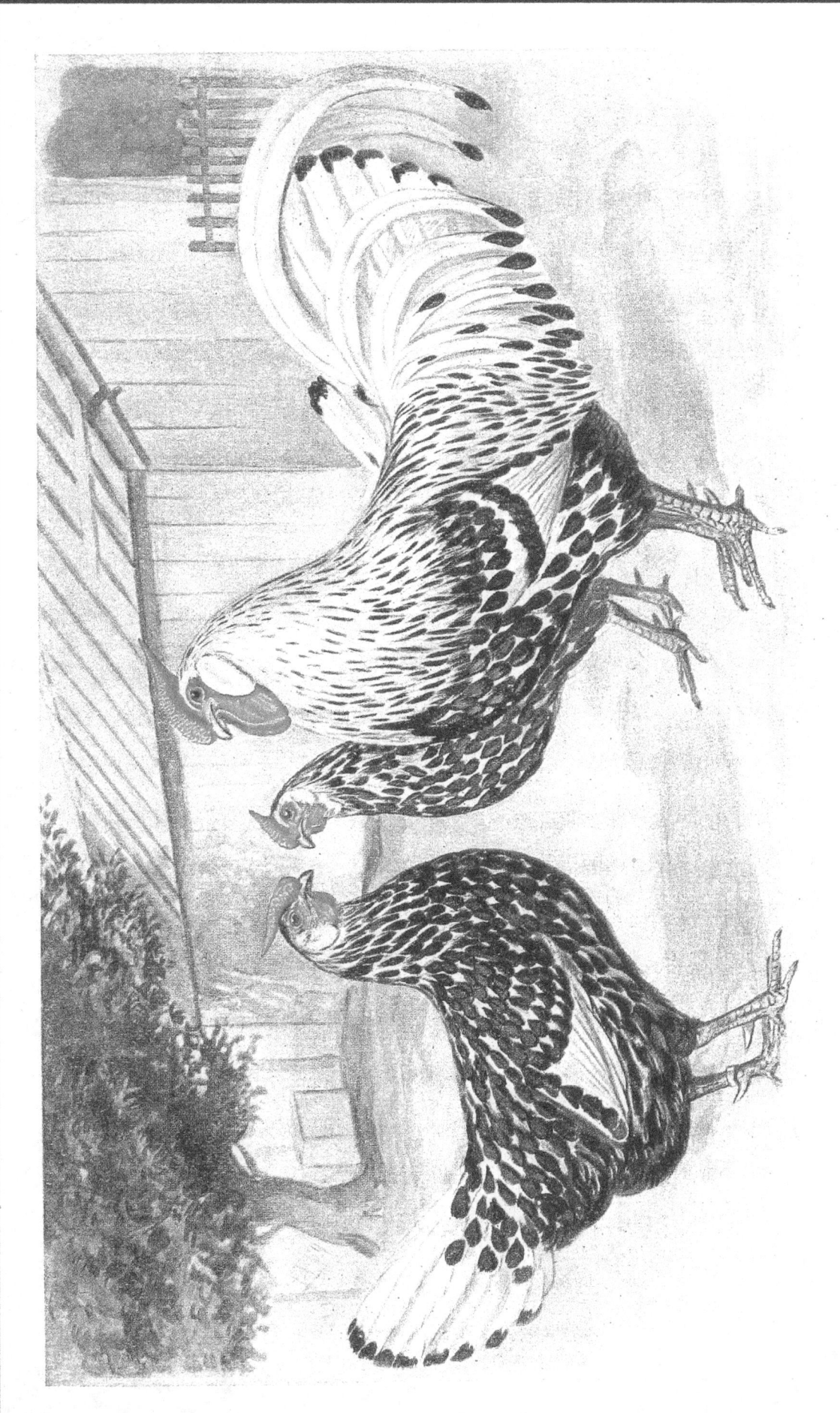

SILVER-SPANGLED HAMBURGS

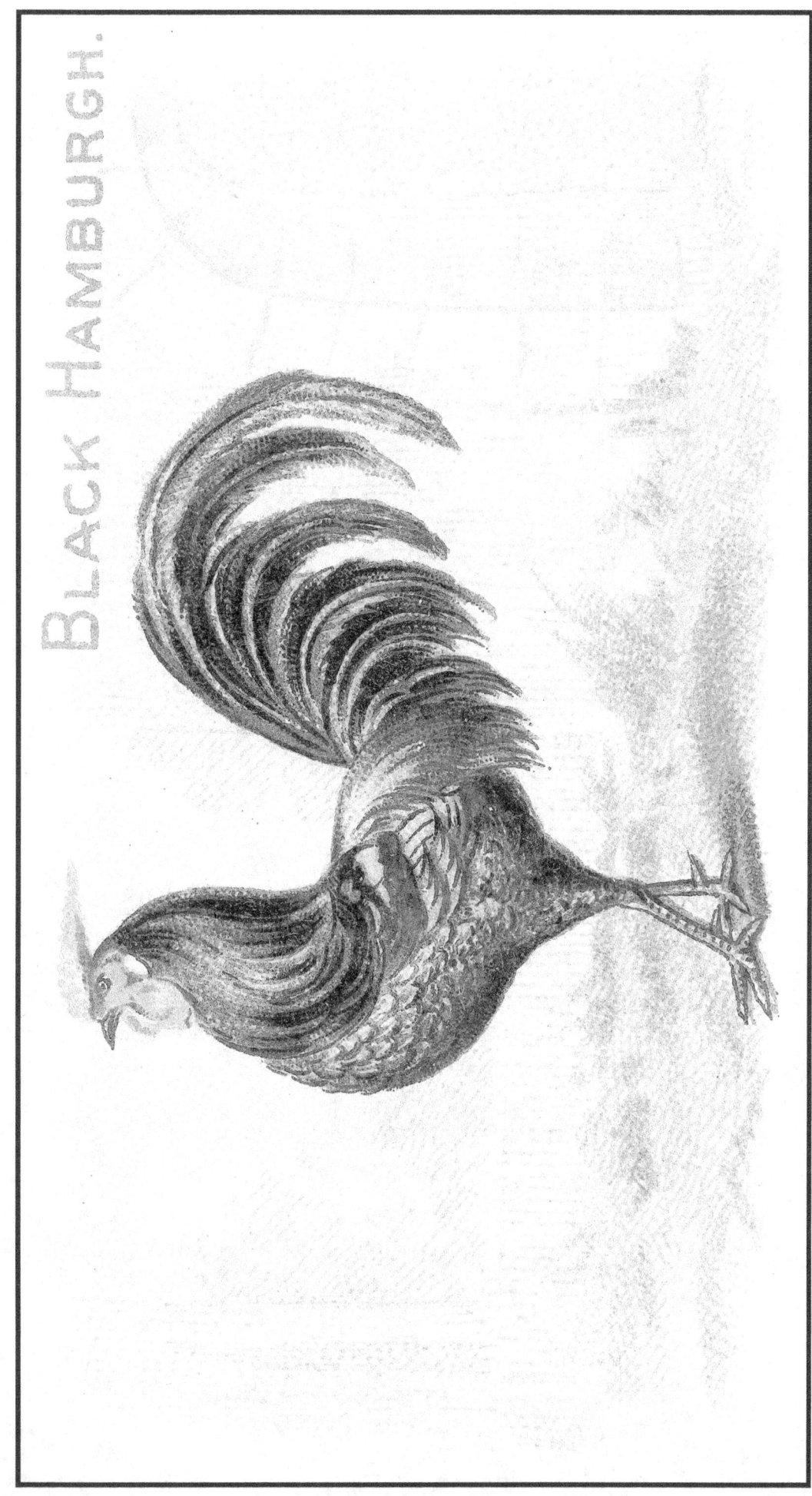

BLACK HAMBURGH.

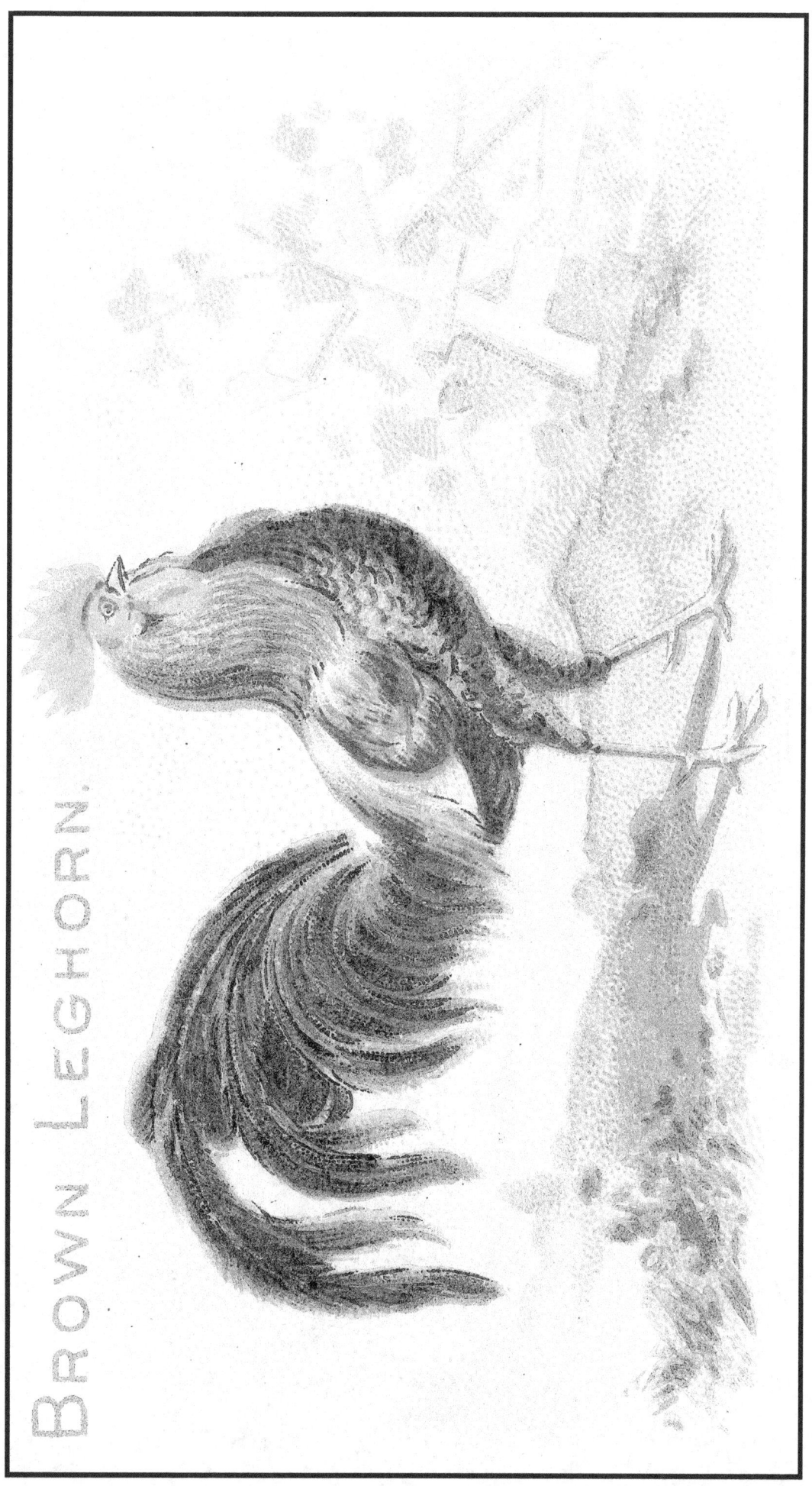

BROWN LEGHORN.

WHITE ORPINGTONS

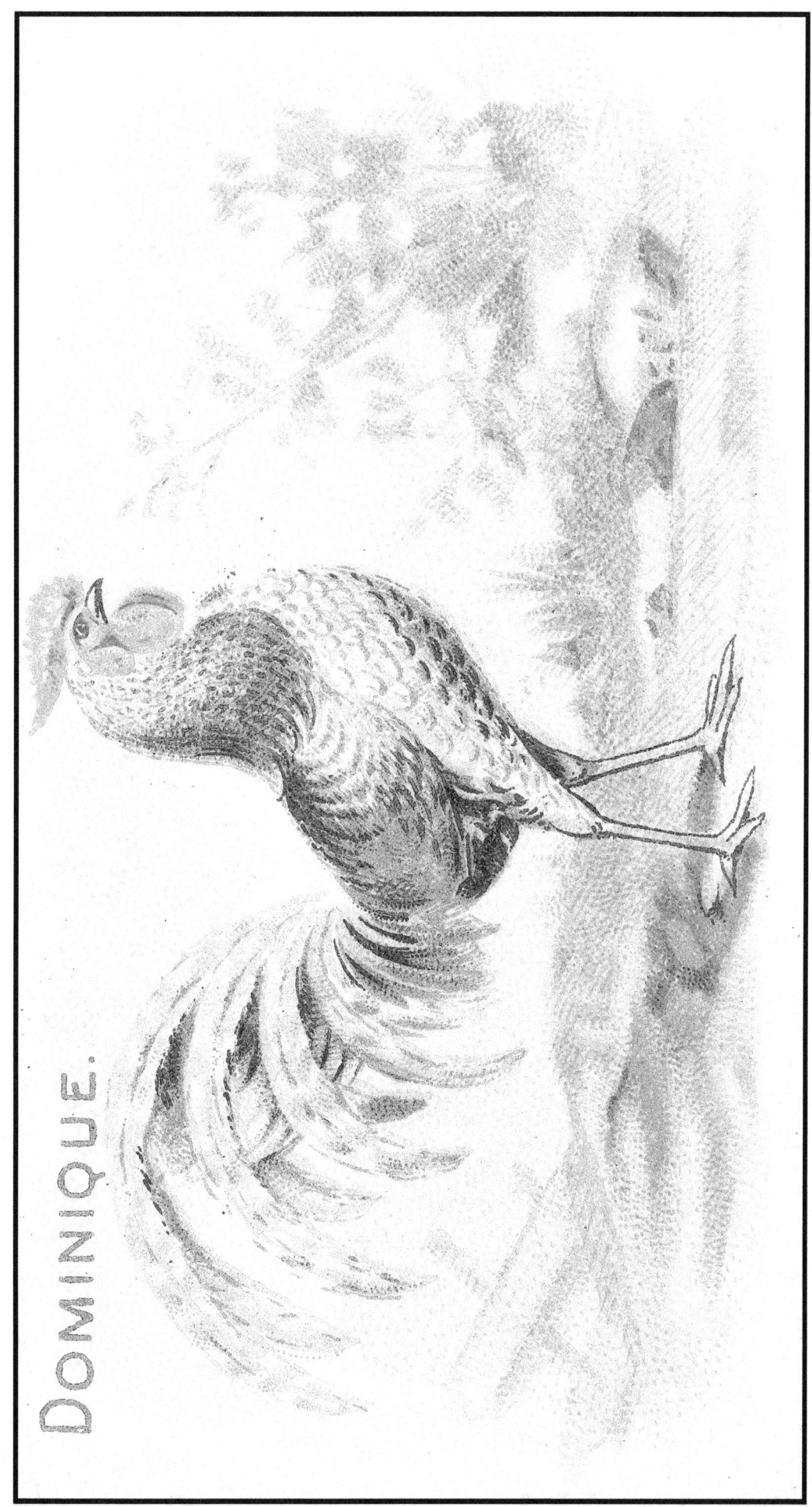

DOMINIQUE.

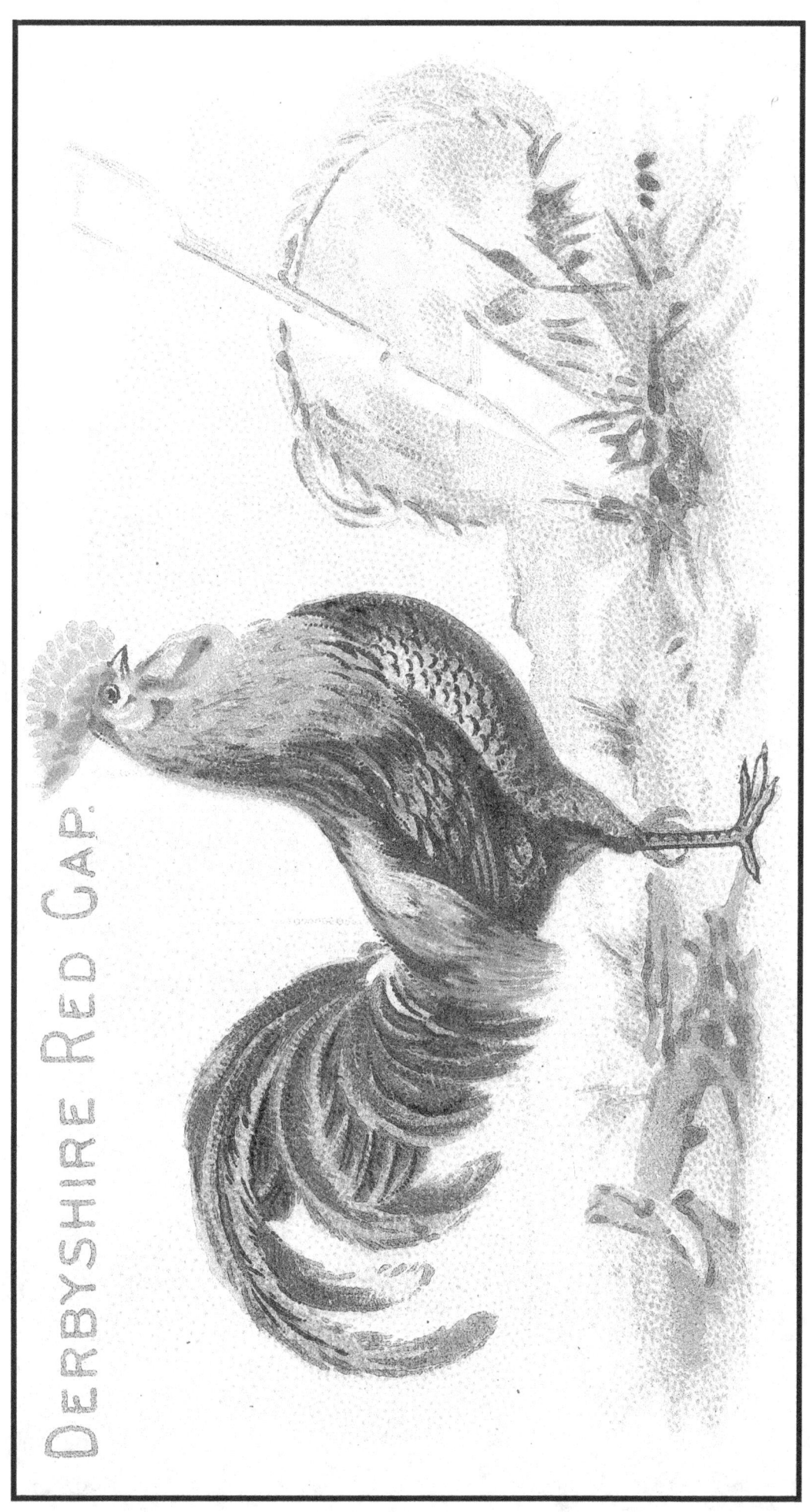

DERBYSHIRE RED CAP.

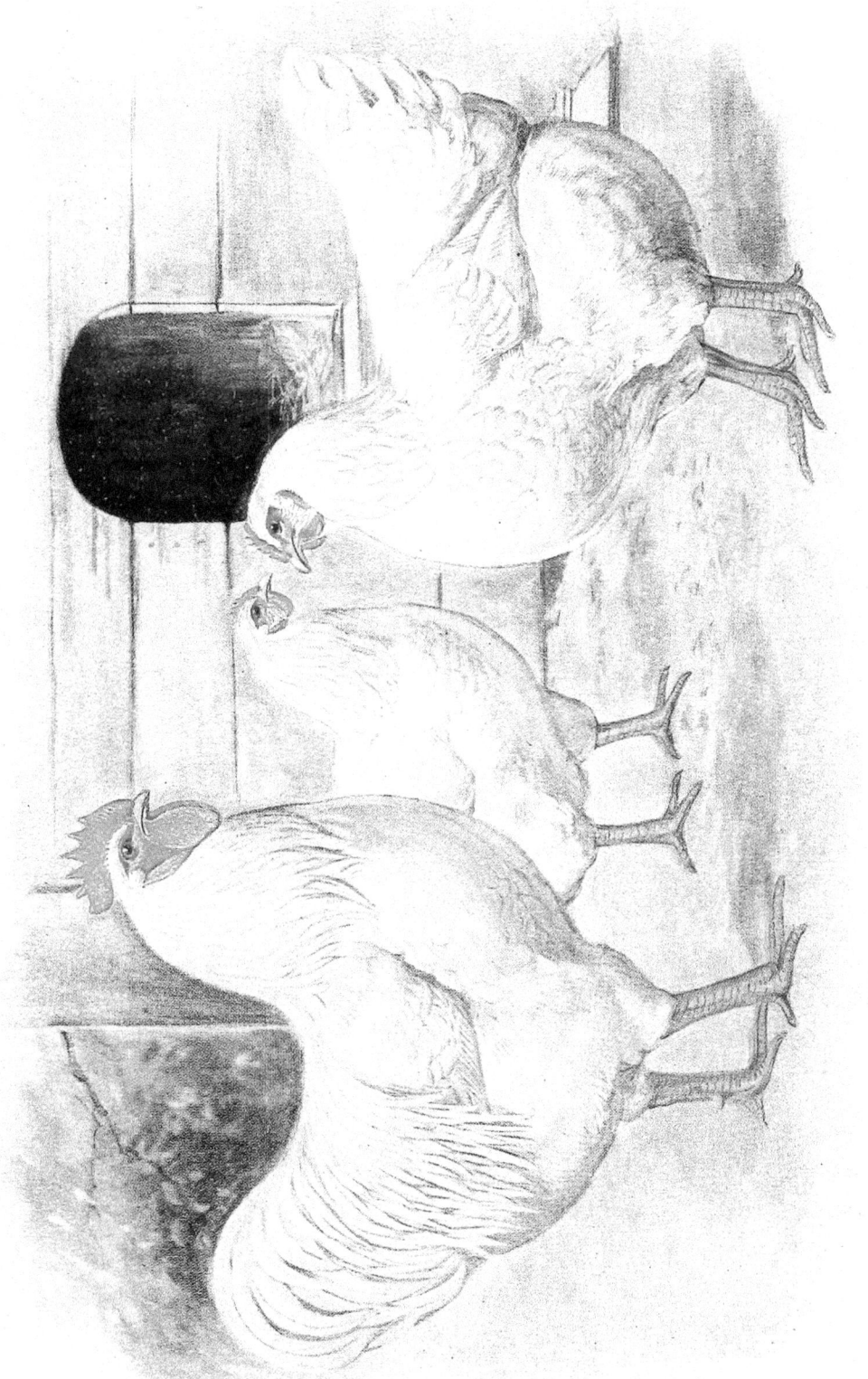

WHITE PLYMOUTH ROCKS

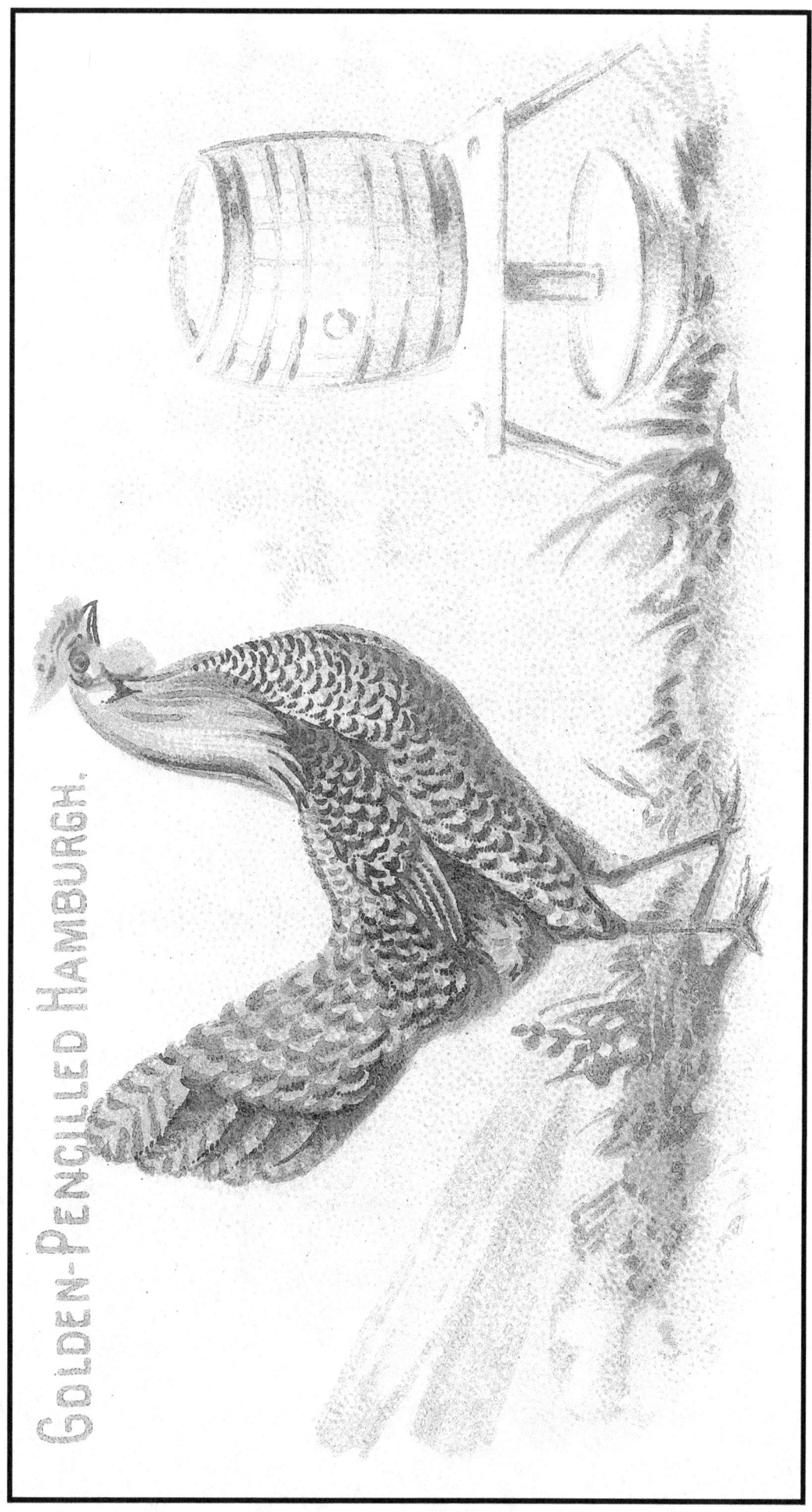

GOLDEN-PENCILLED HAMBURGH.

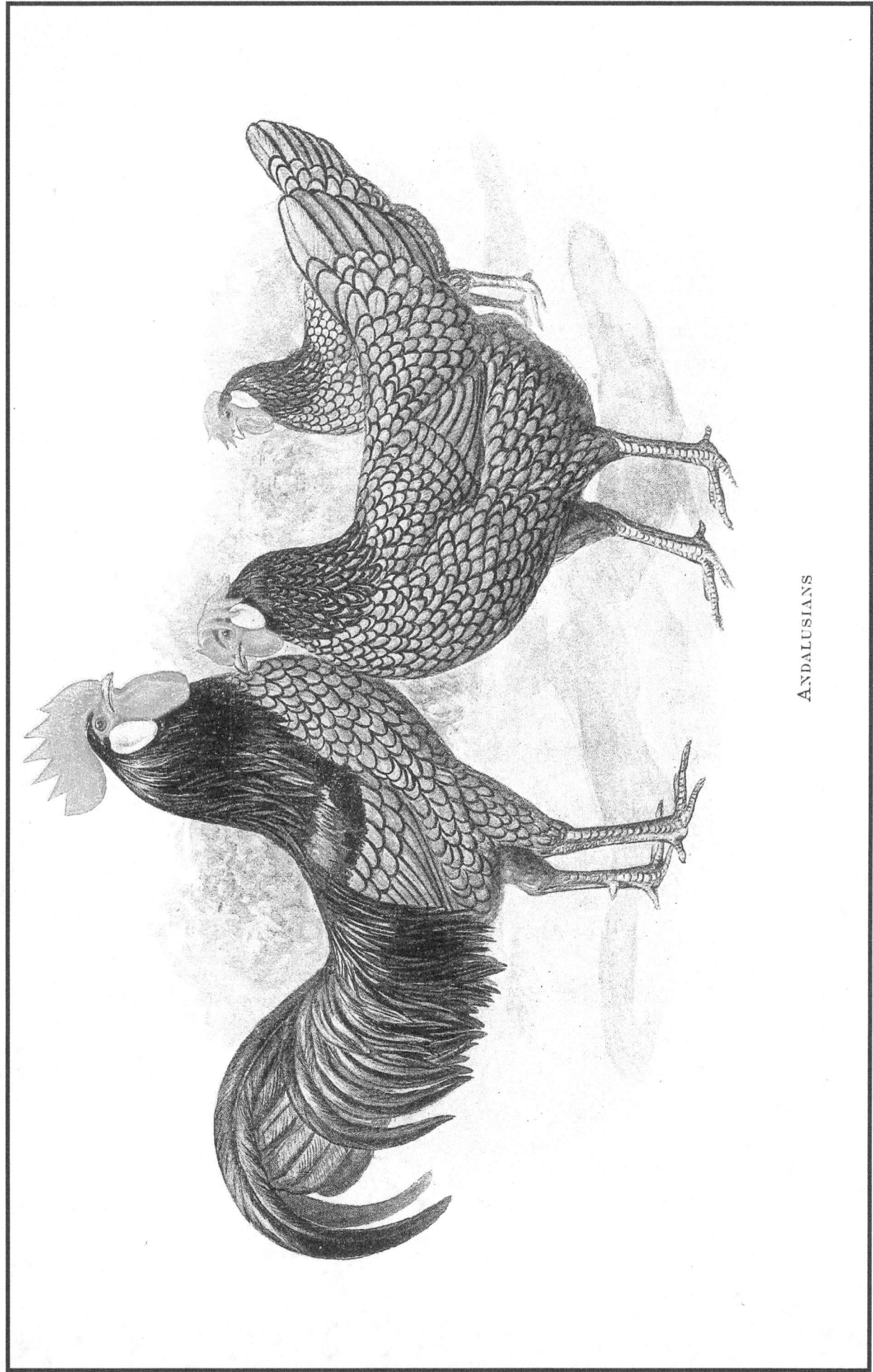

ANDALUSIANS

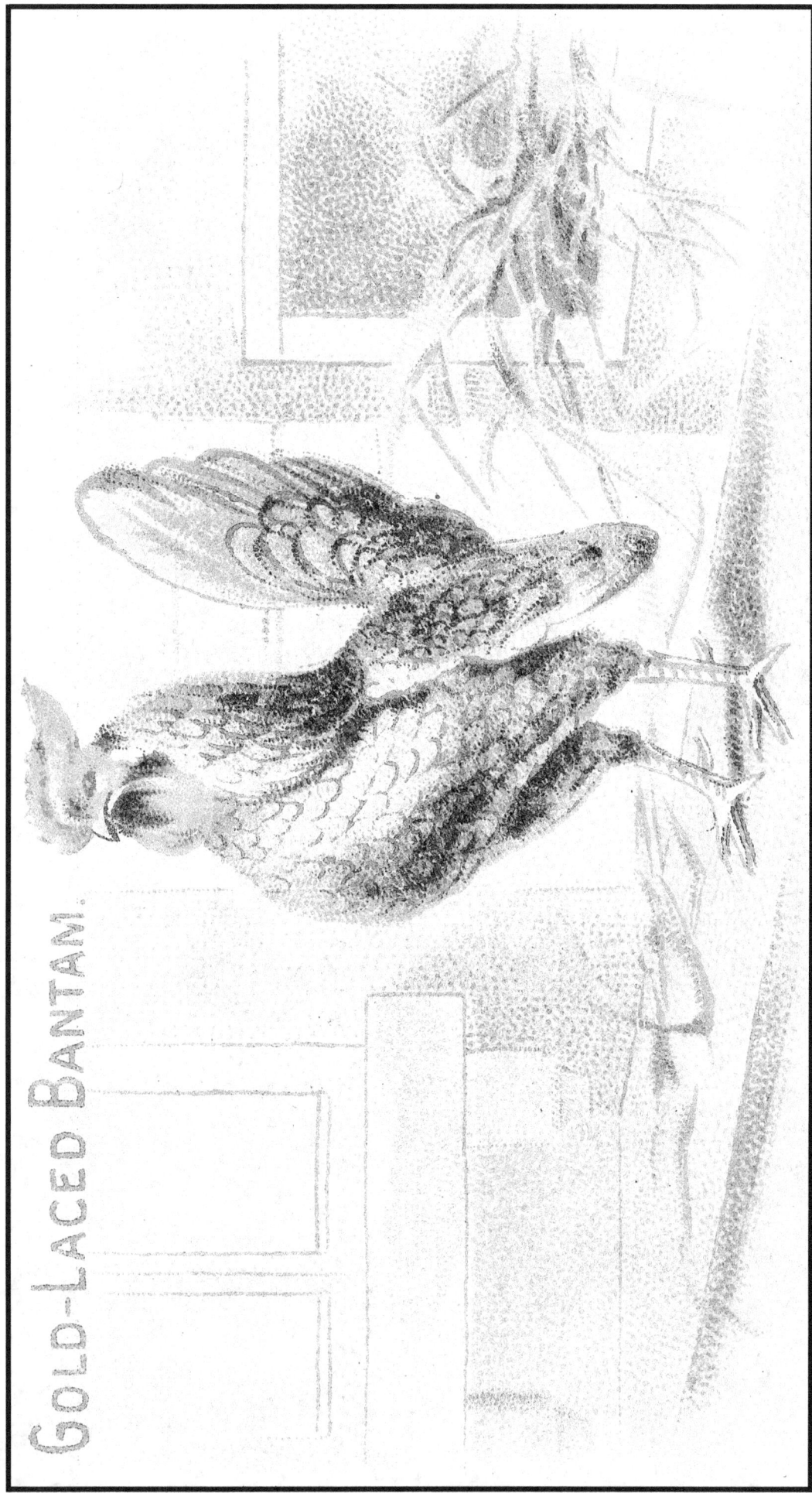

GOLD-LACED BANTAM.

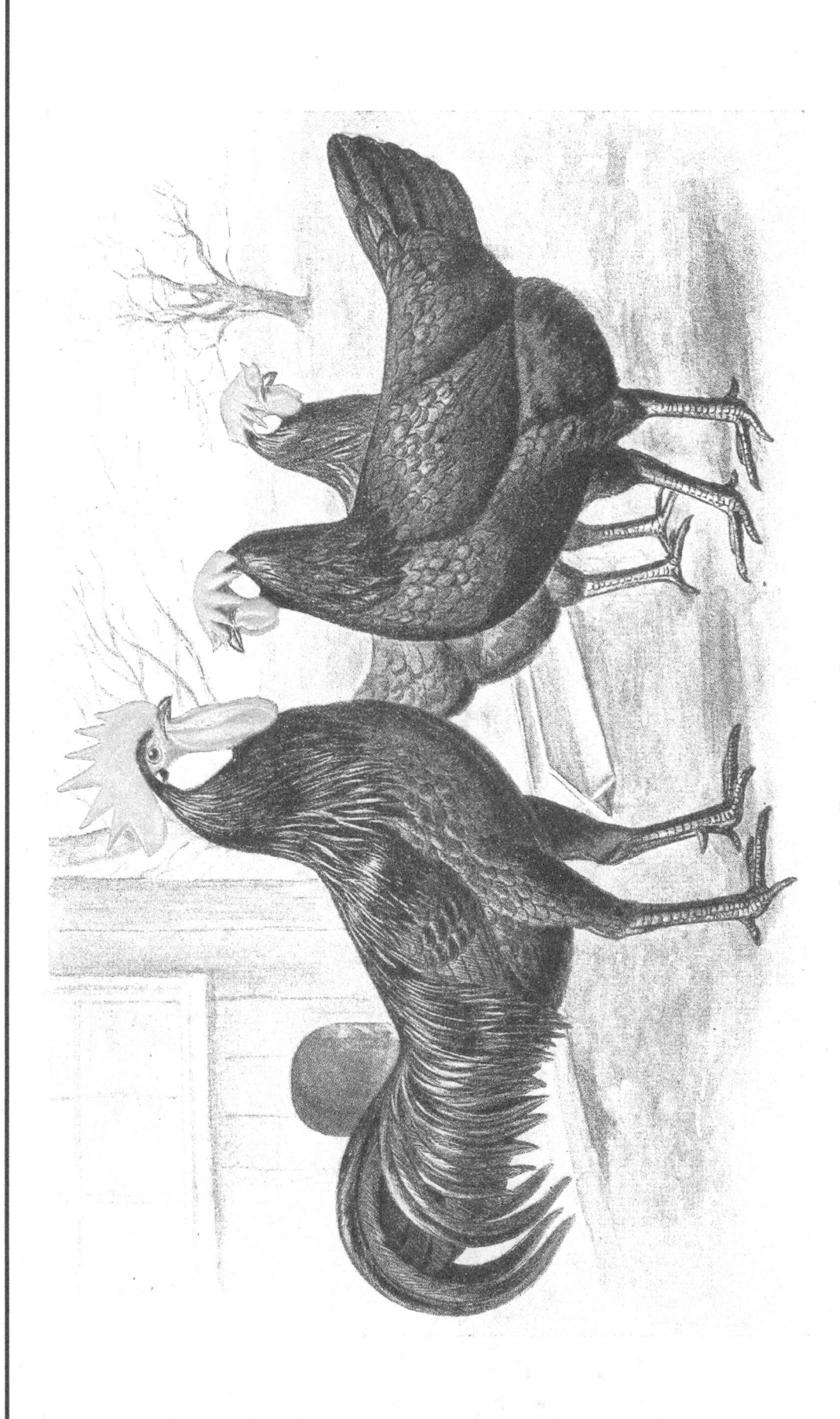

Single-Comb Black Minorcas

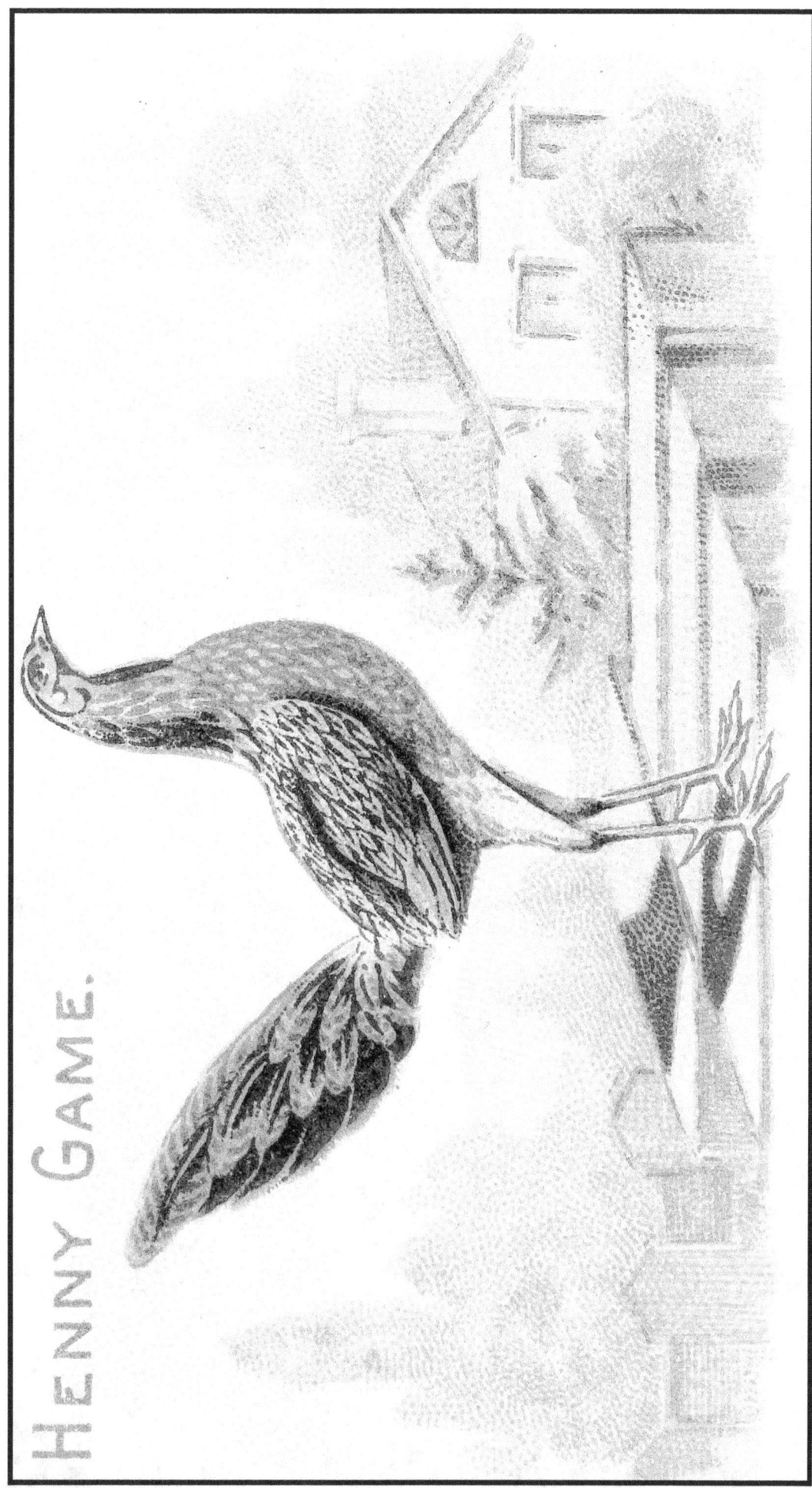

HENNY GAME.

POLISH BANTAMS

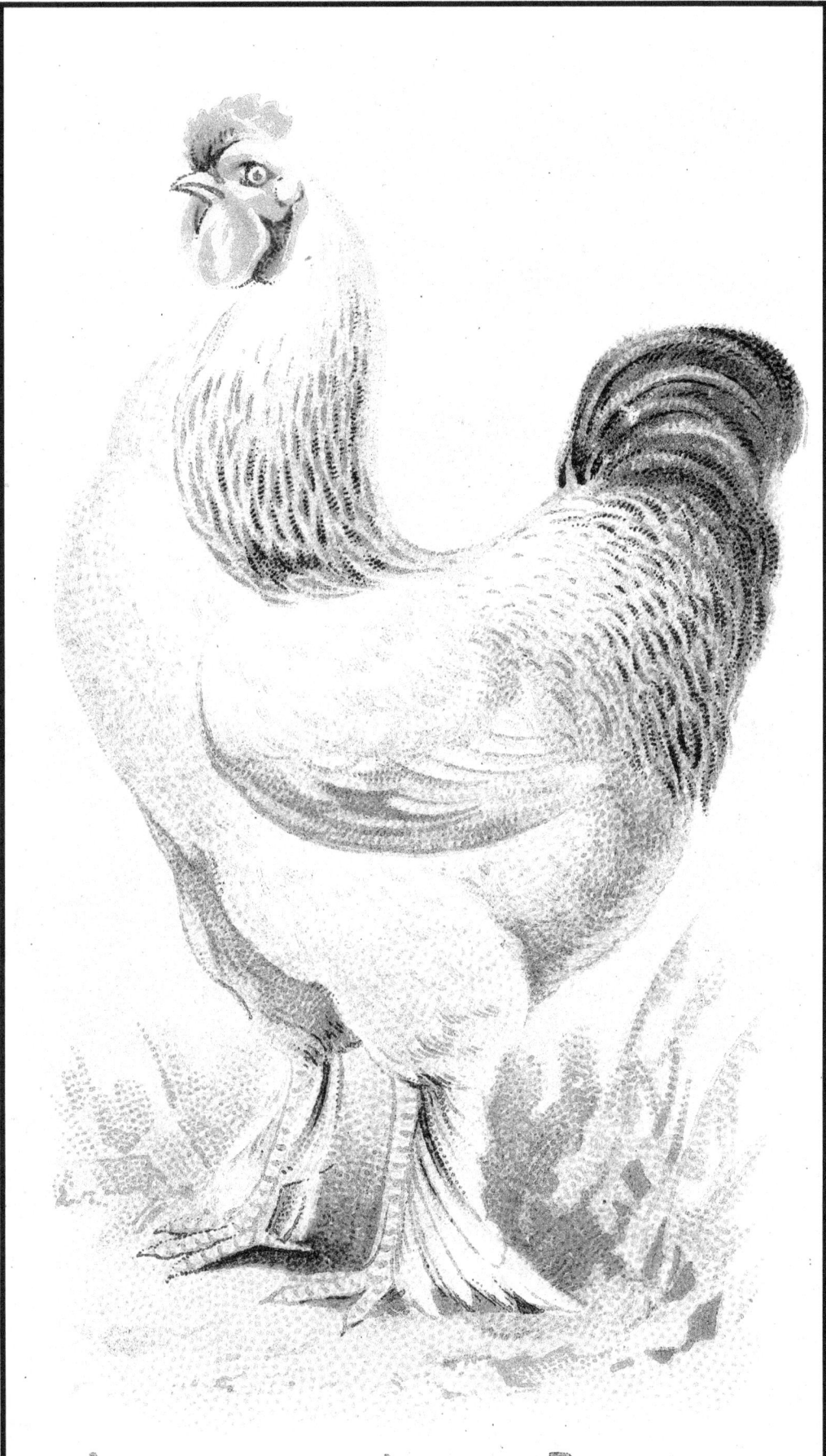

AMERICAN LIGHT BRAHMA.

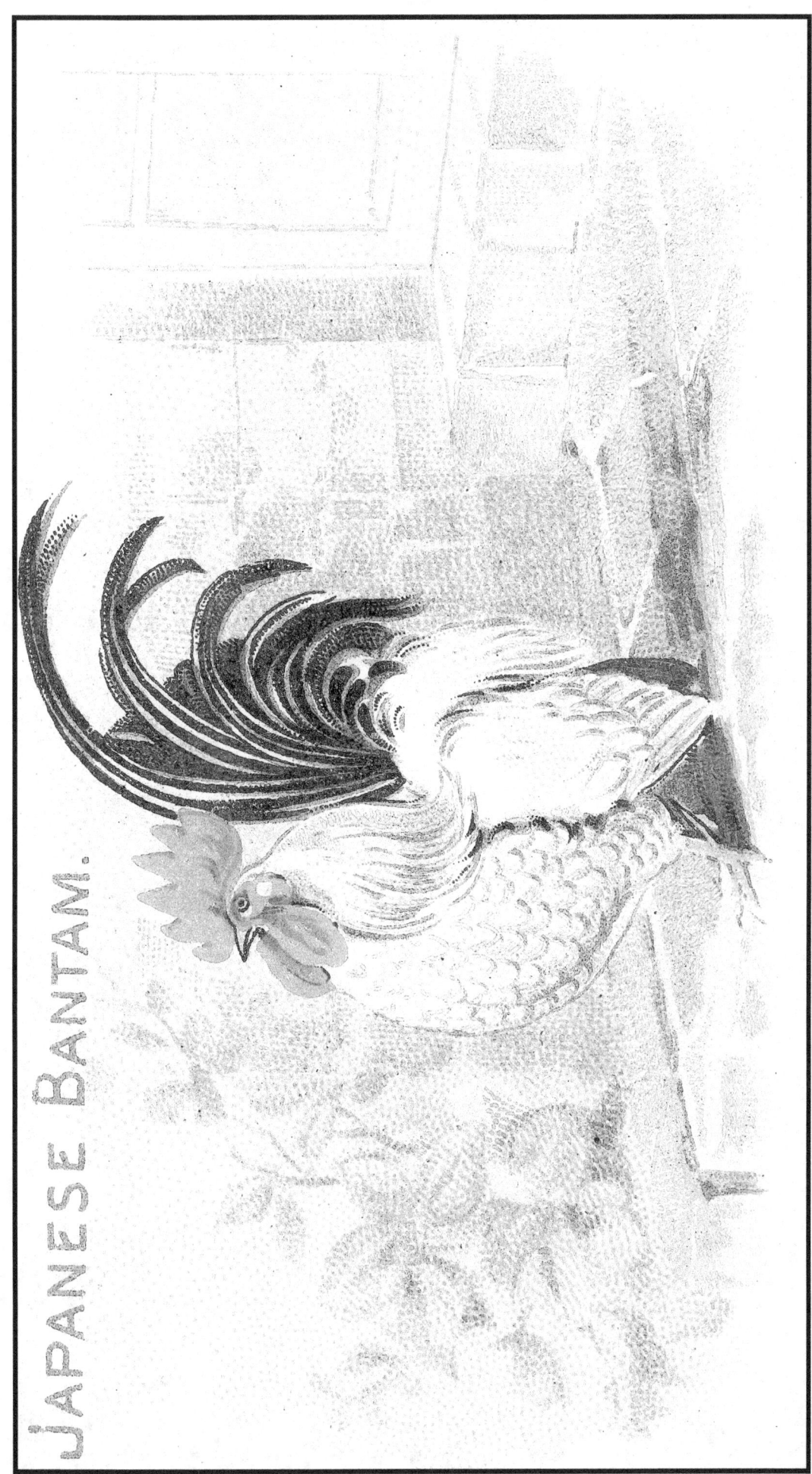

JAPANESE BANTAM.

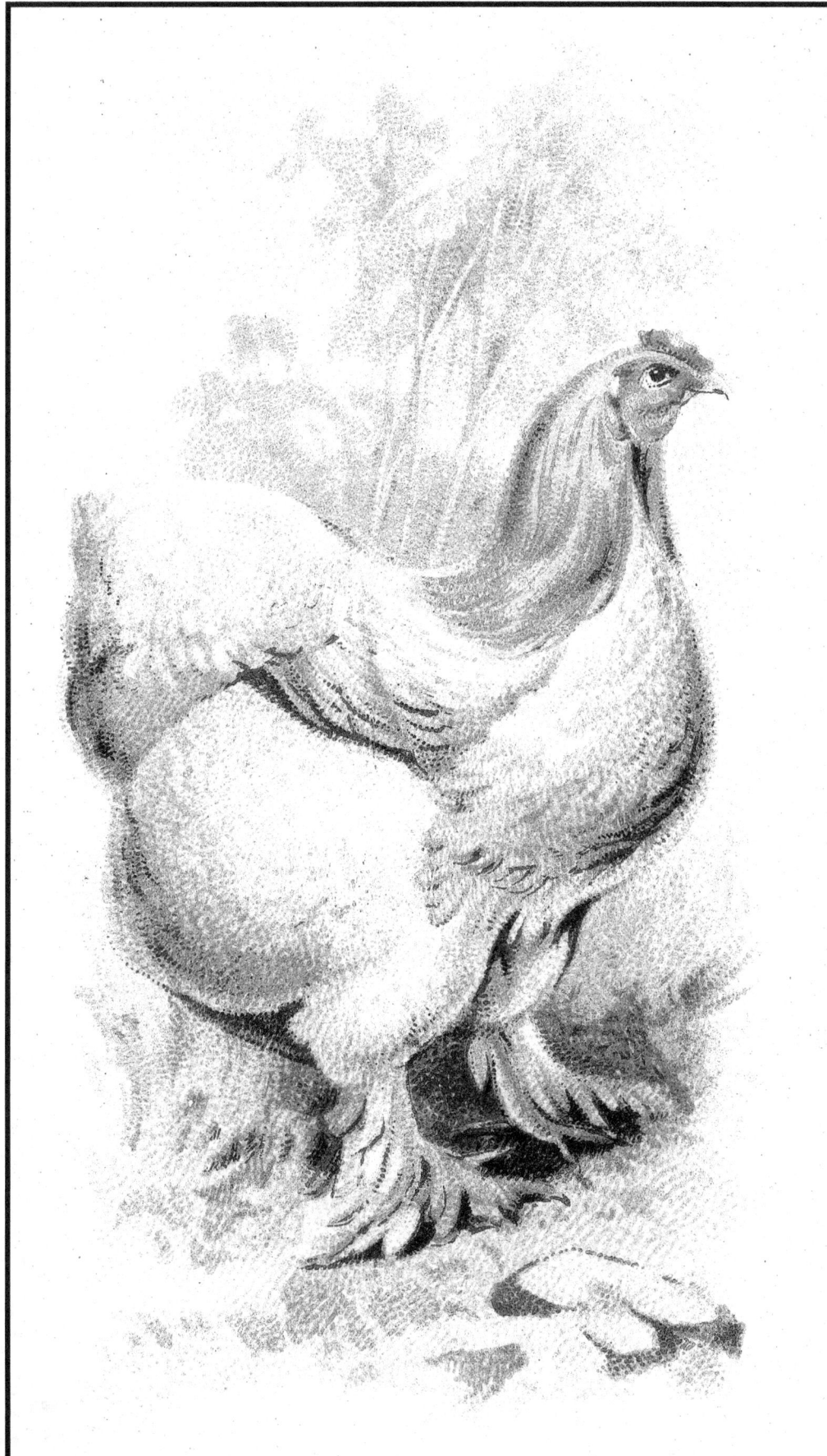

BUFF COCHIN CHINA HEN.

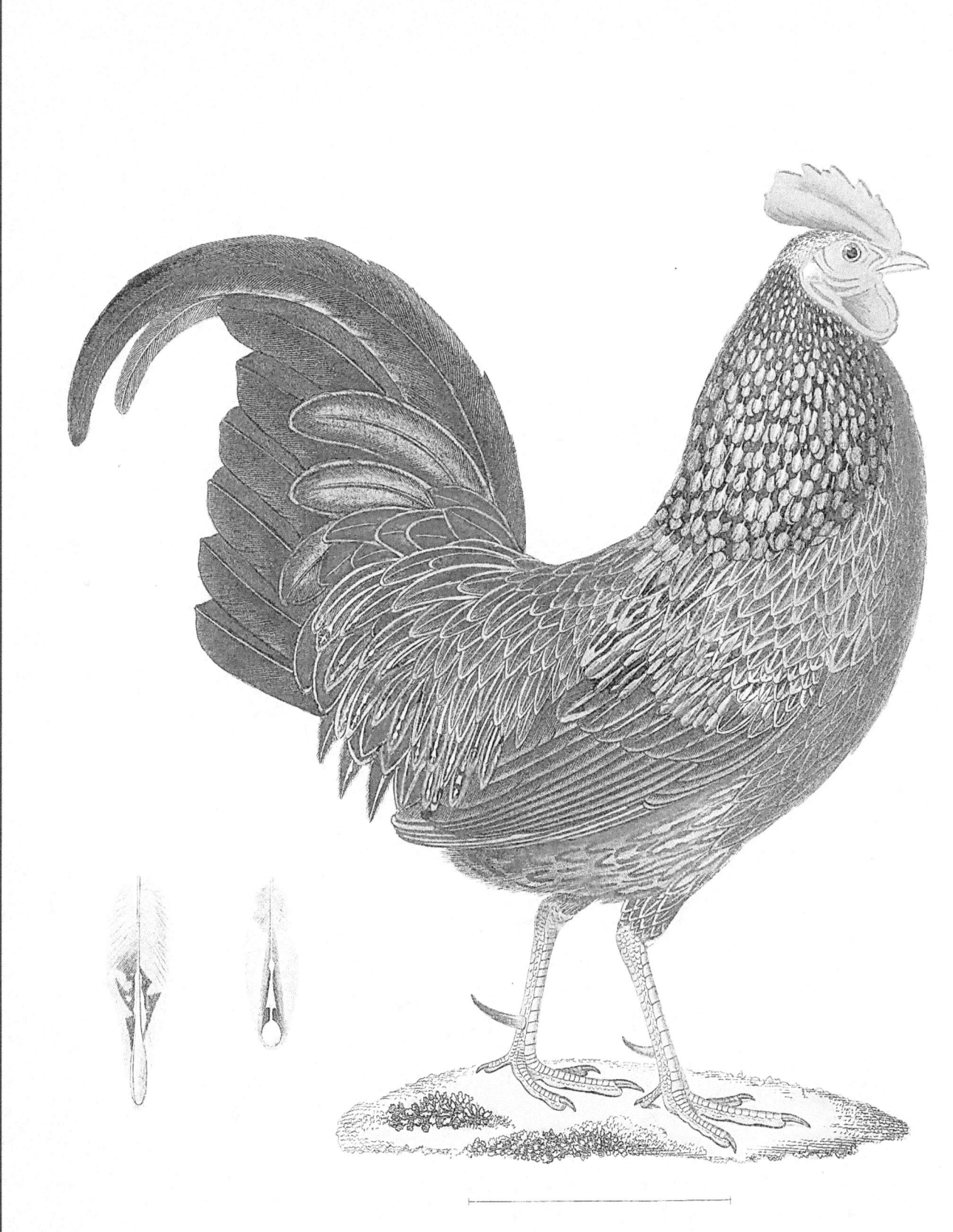

Coq sonneral.

MALAY COCK.

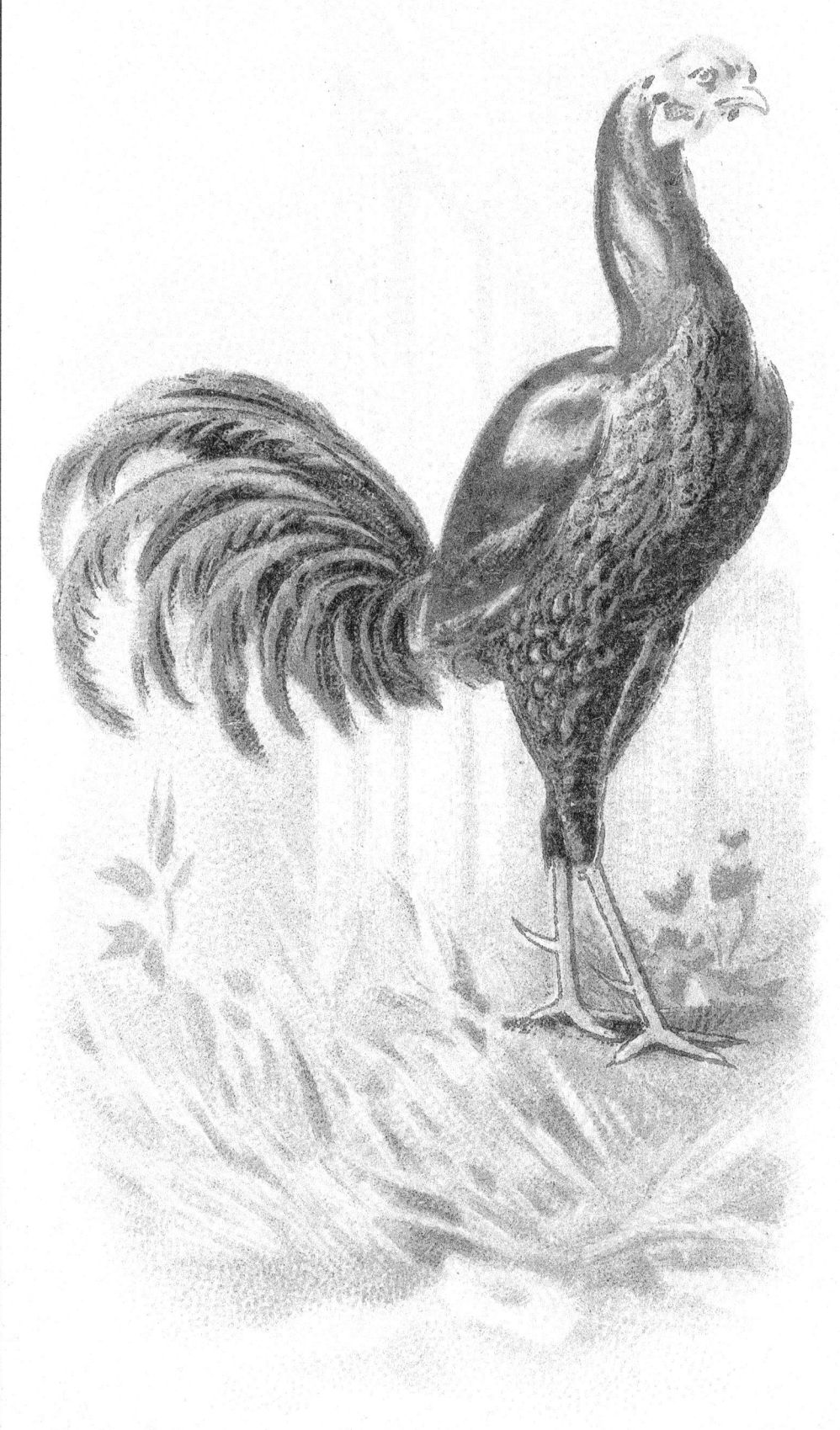

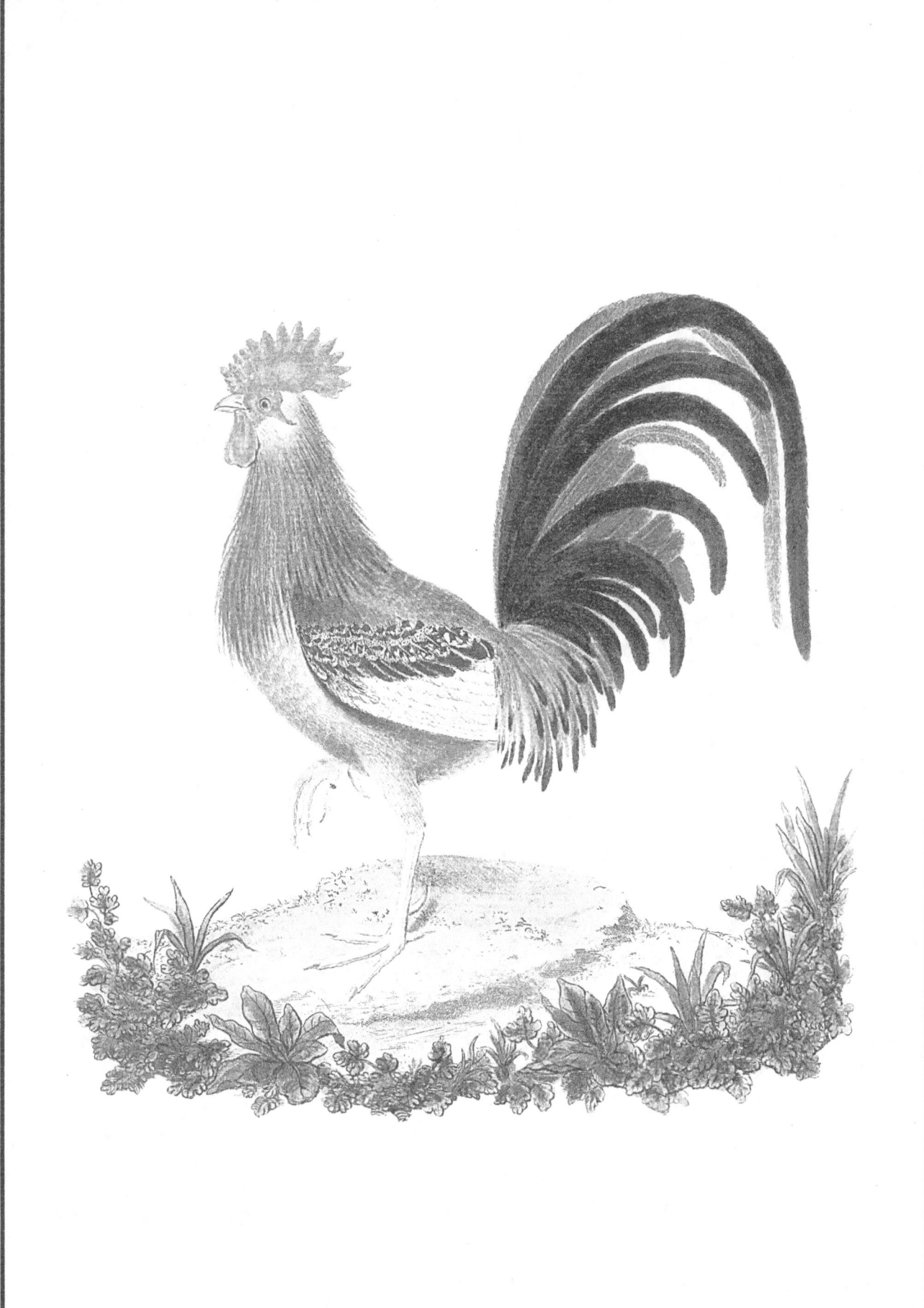

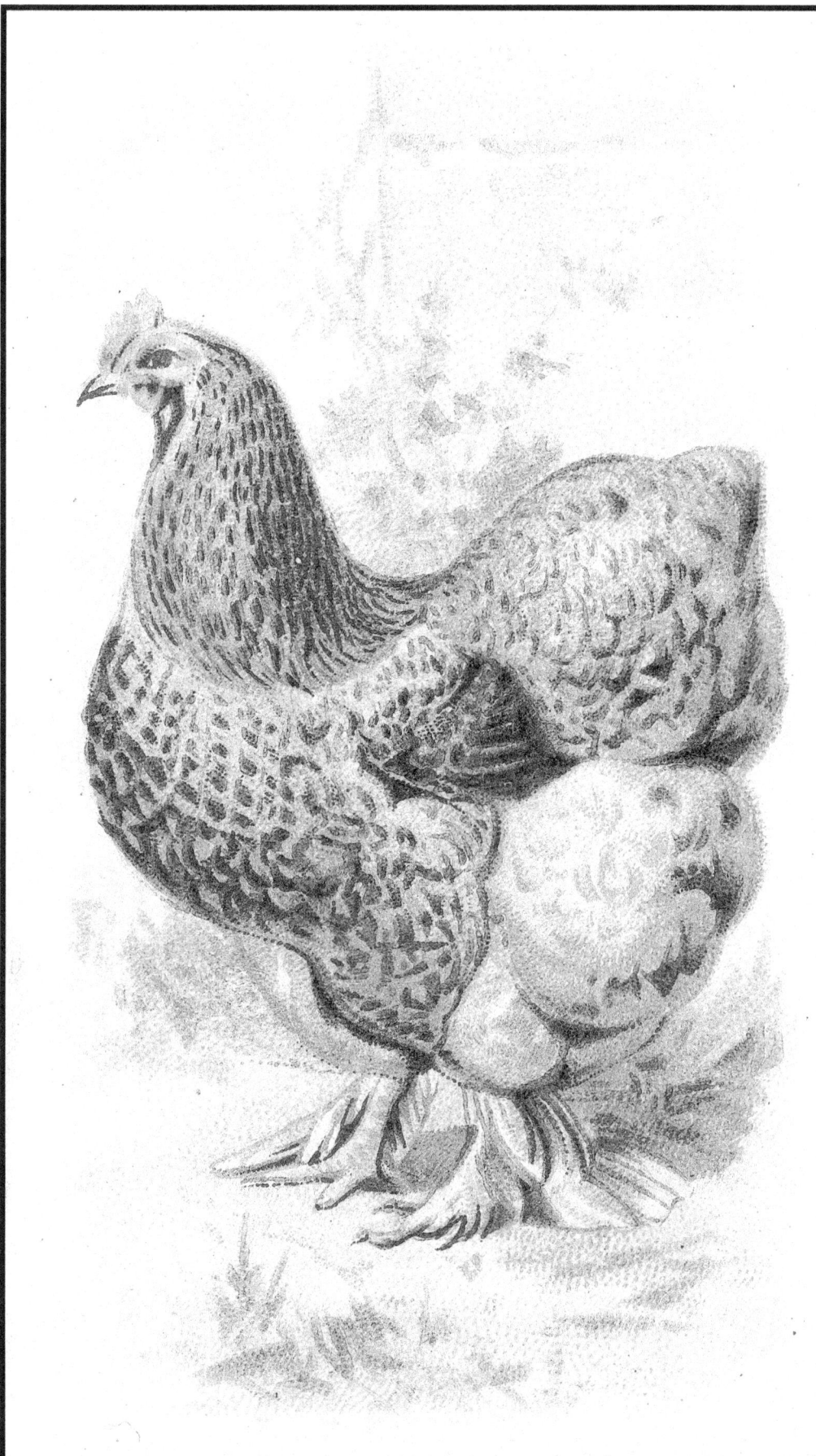

PARTRIDGE COCHIN HEN.

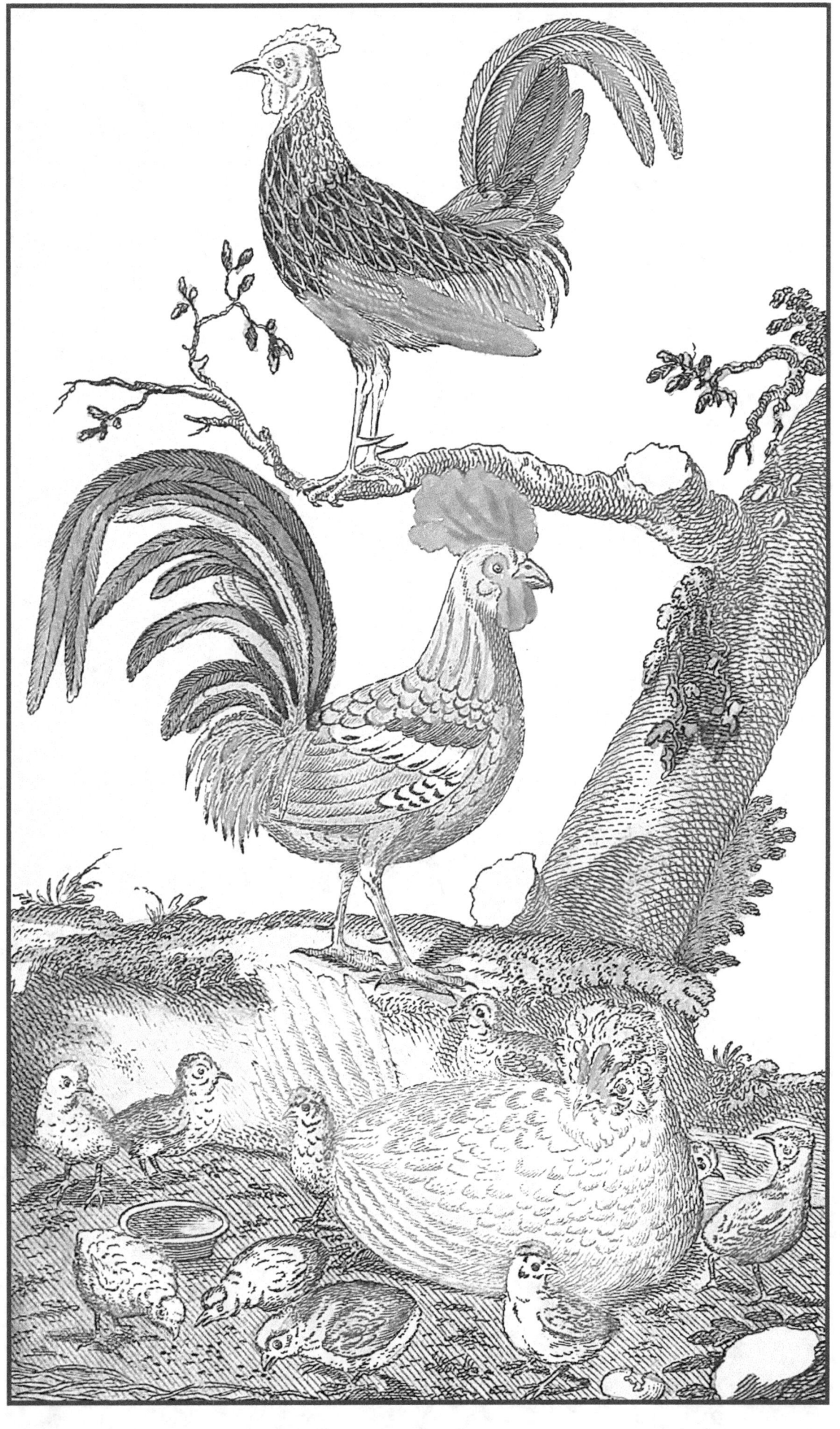

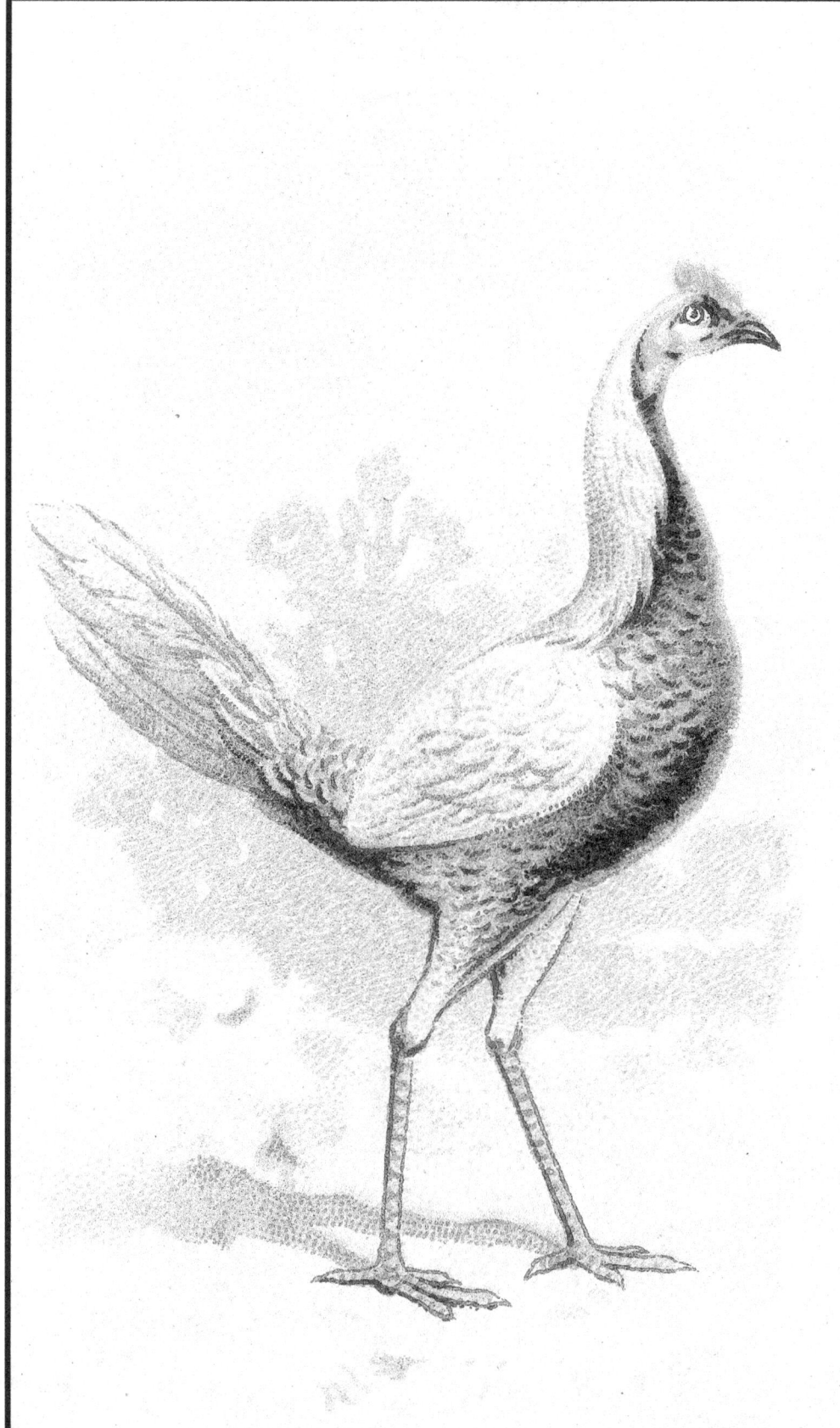

PILE GAME HEN.

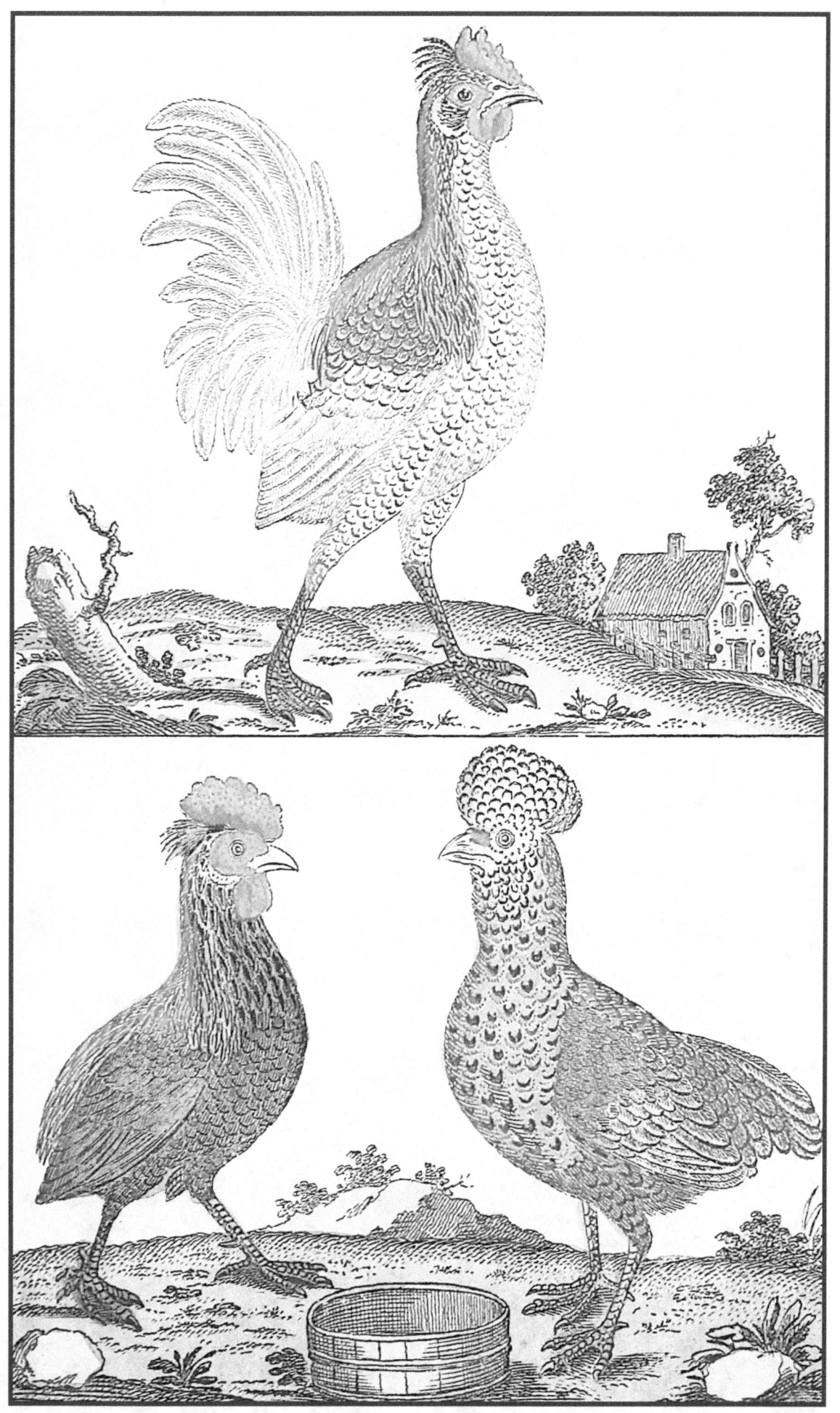

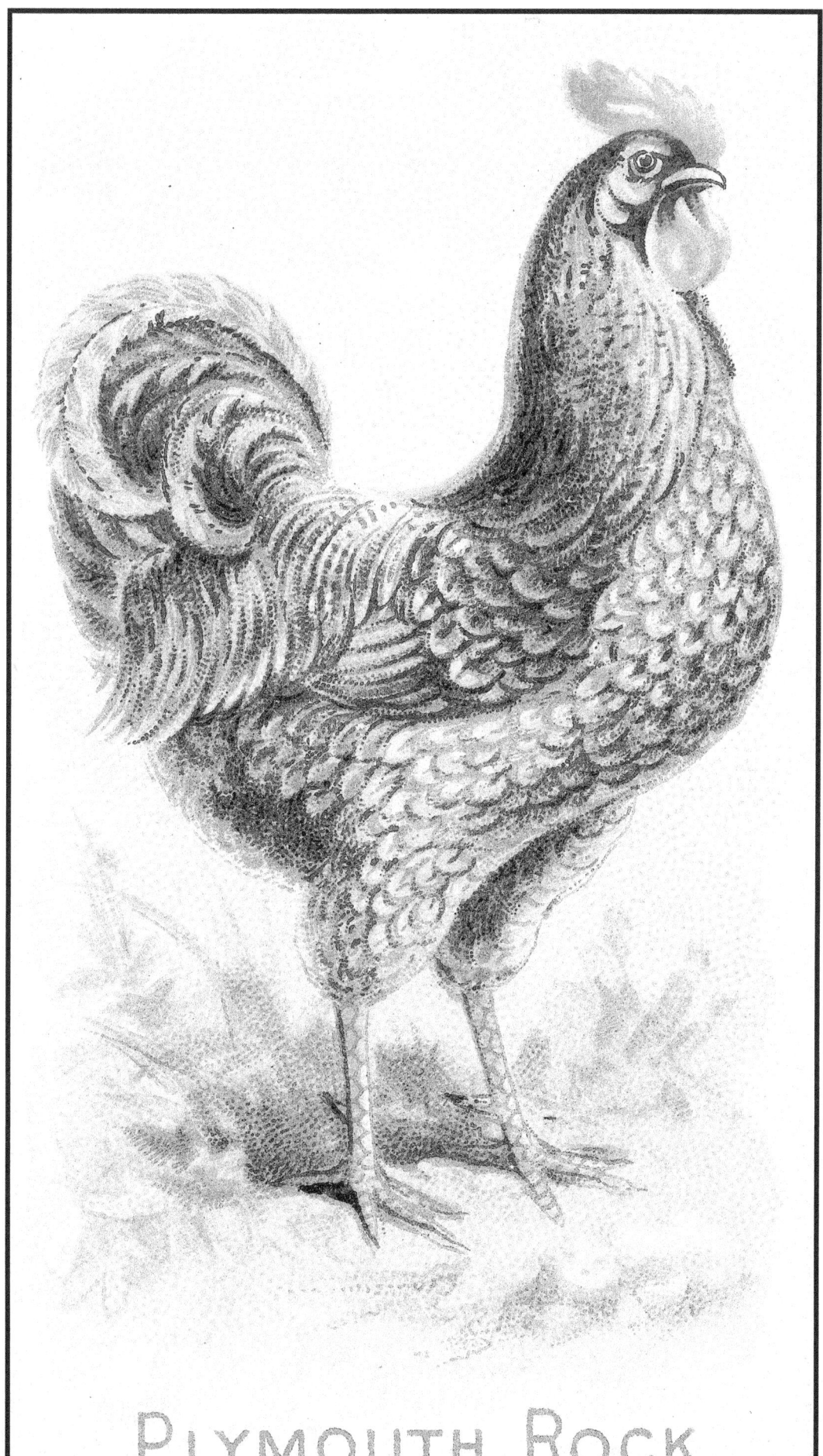

PLYMOUTH ROCK.

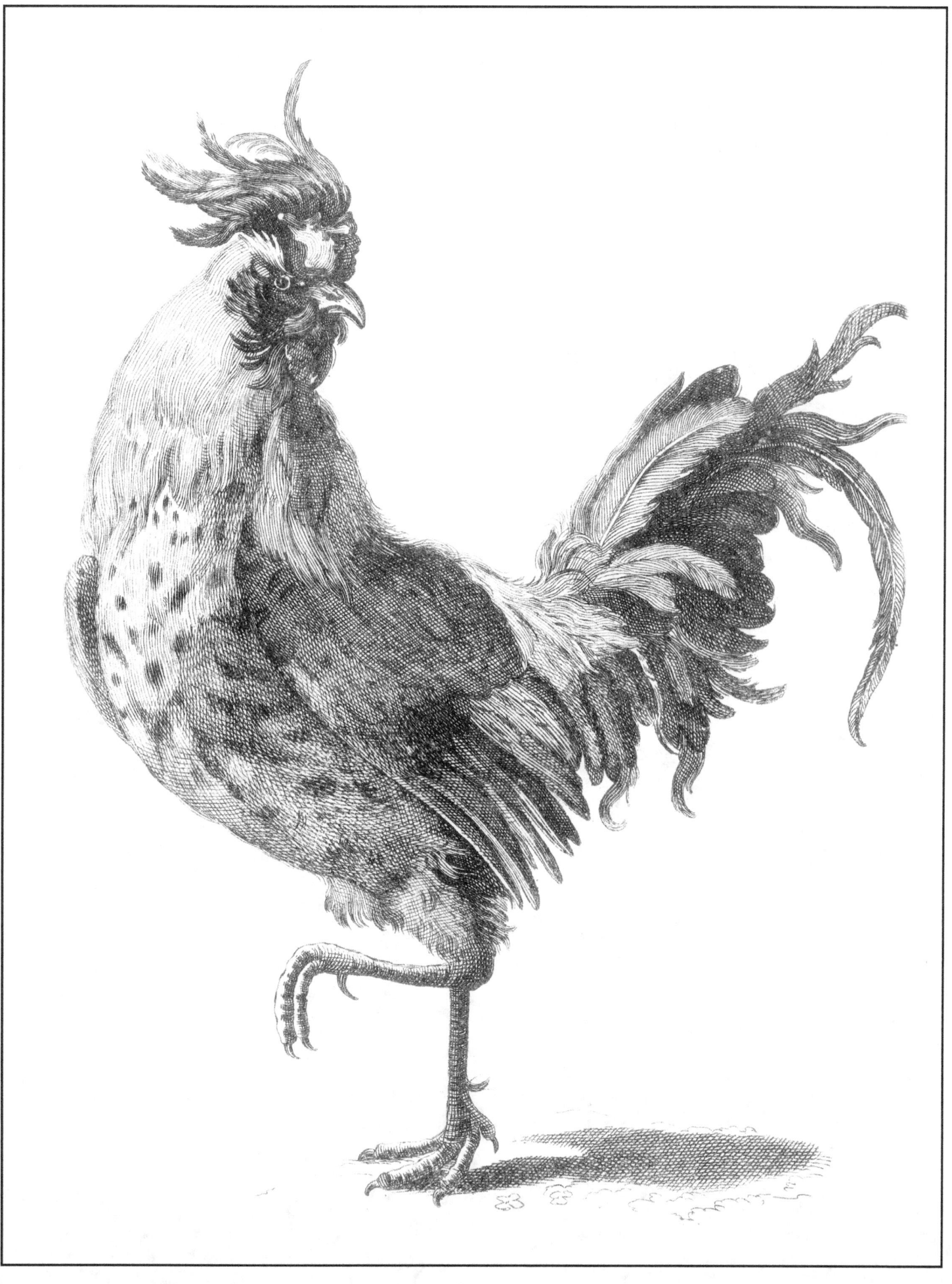

4ᵐᵉ Ordre. GALLINACÉS . FAISANS. Coq domestique . (Gallus domesticus , Brisé ;) 1/7 de grand. nat.

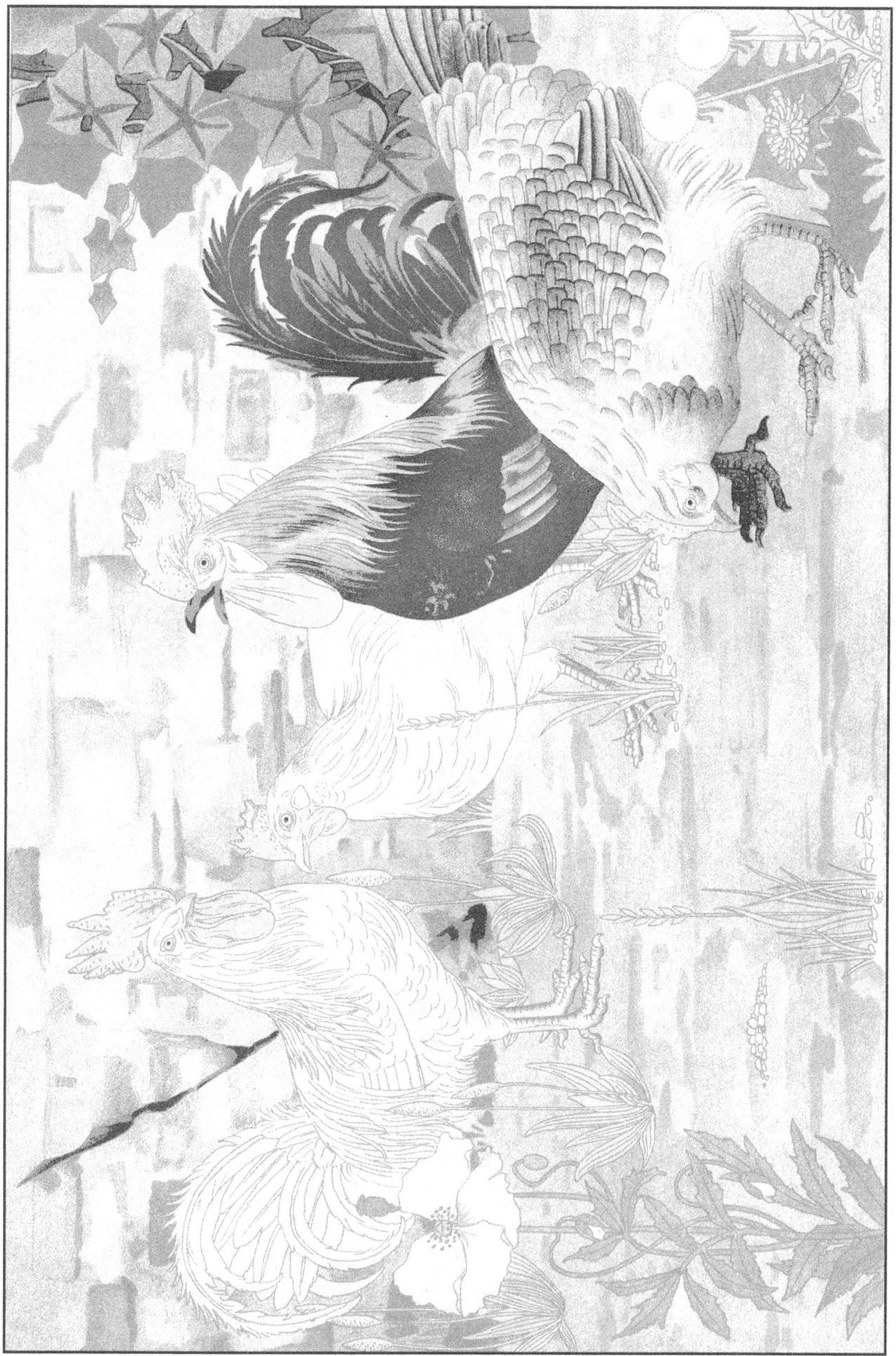

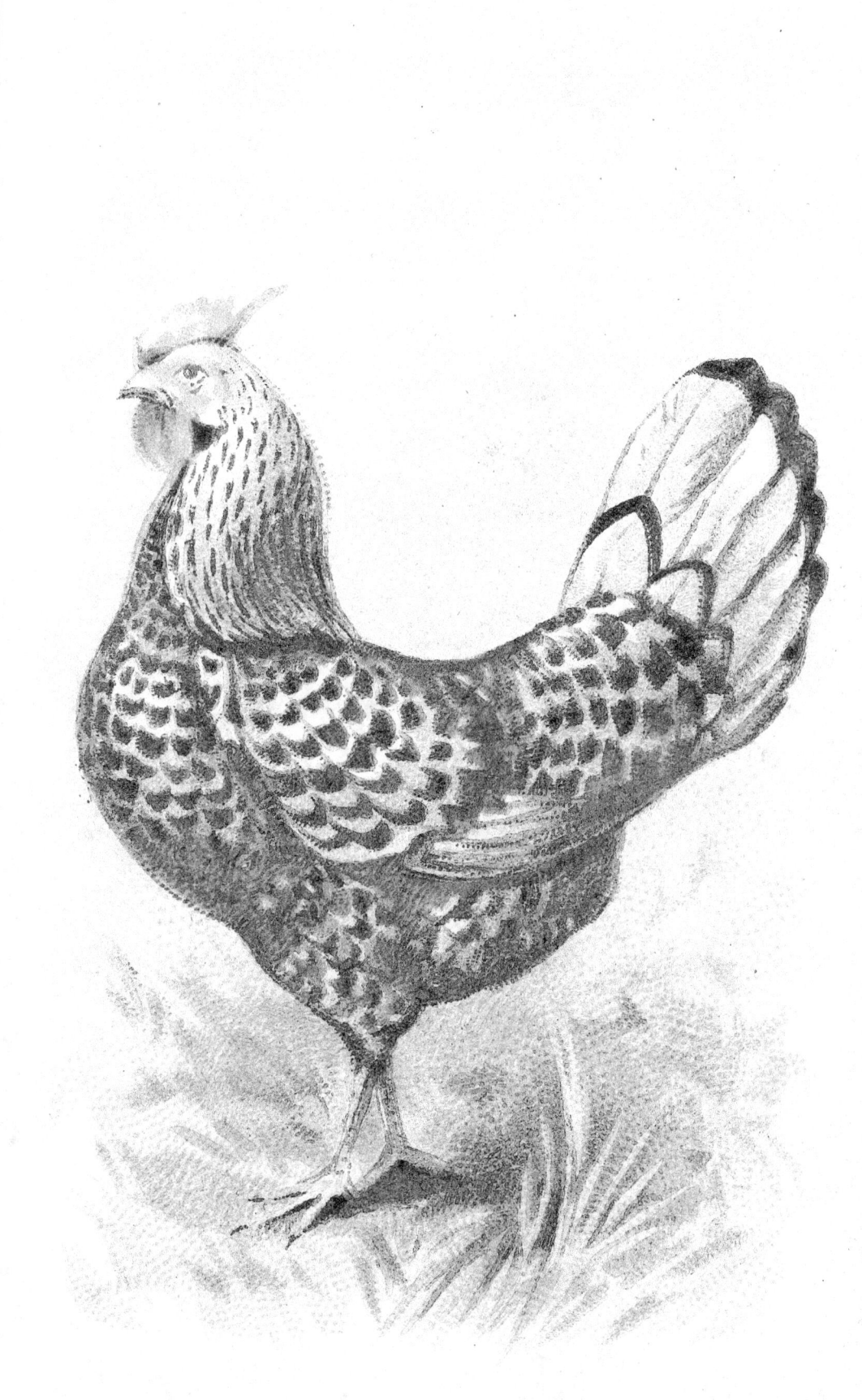

SILVER-SPANGLED HAMBURGH.

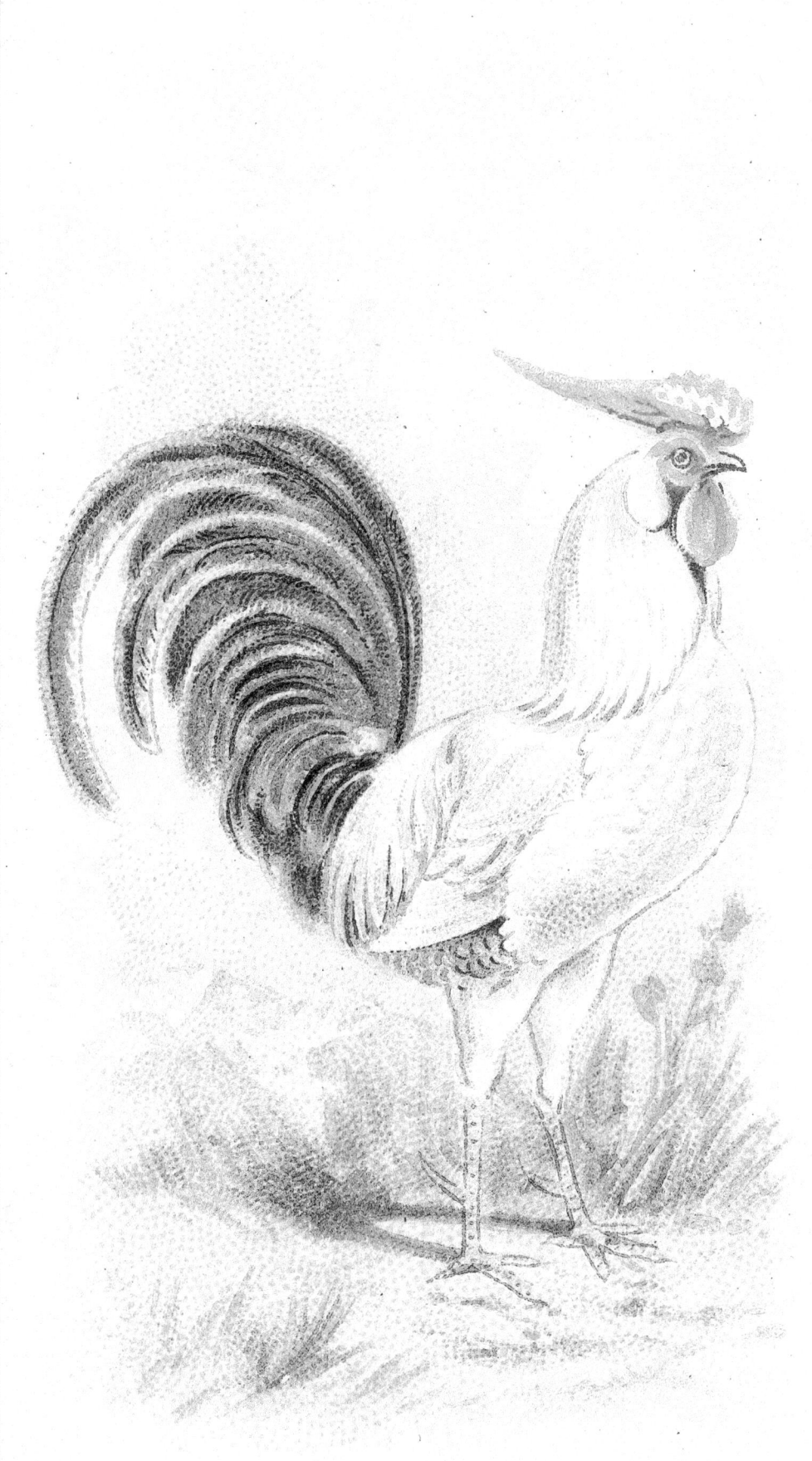

SILVER-PENCILLED HAMBURGH.

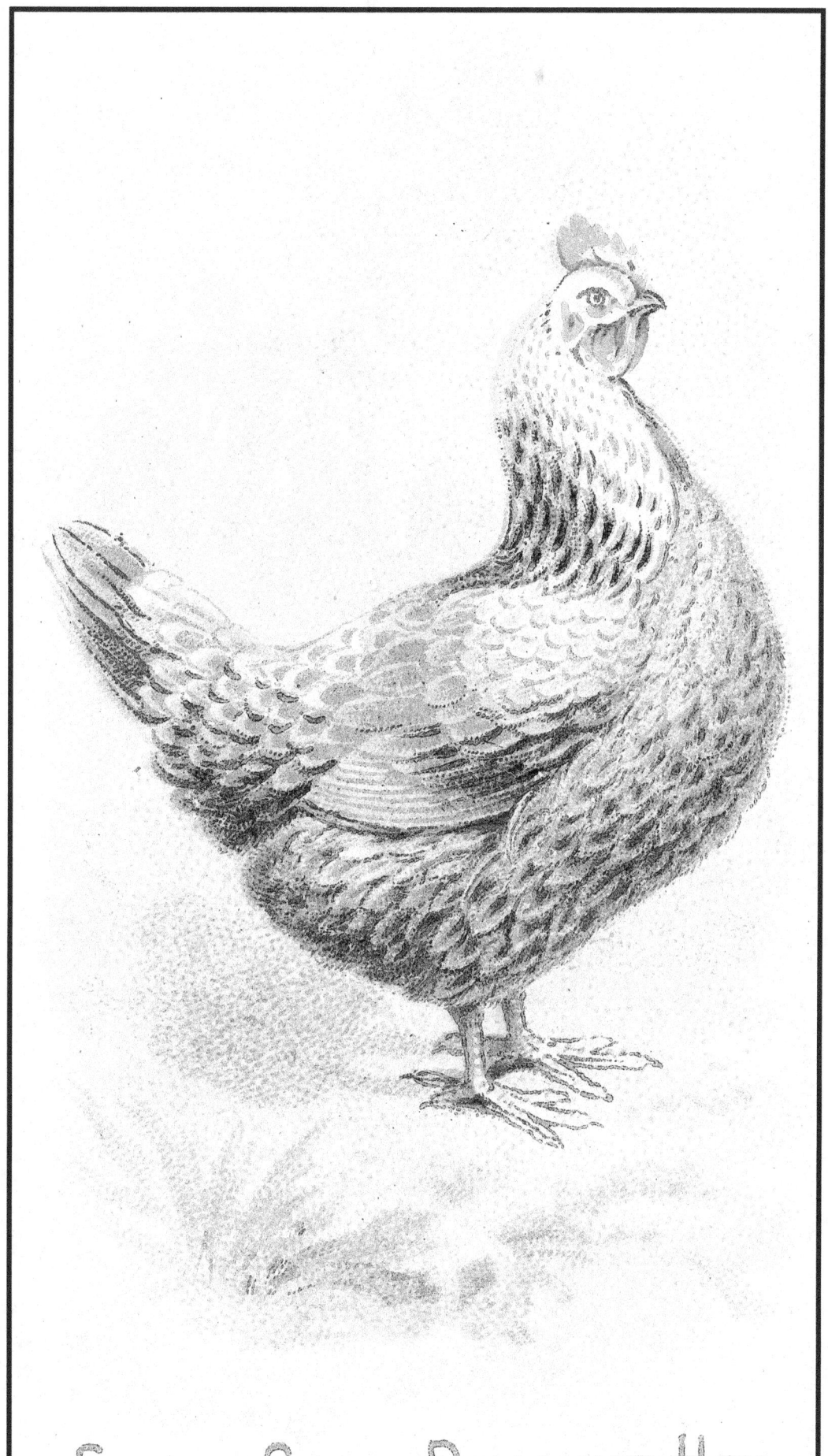

SILVER-GREY DORKING HEN.

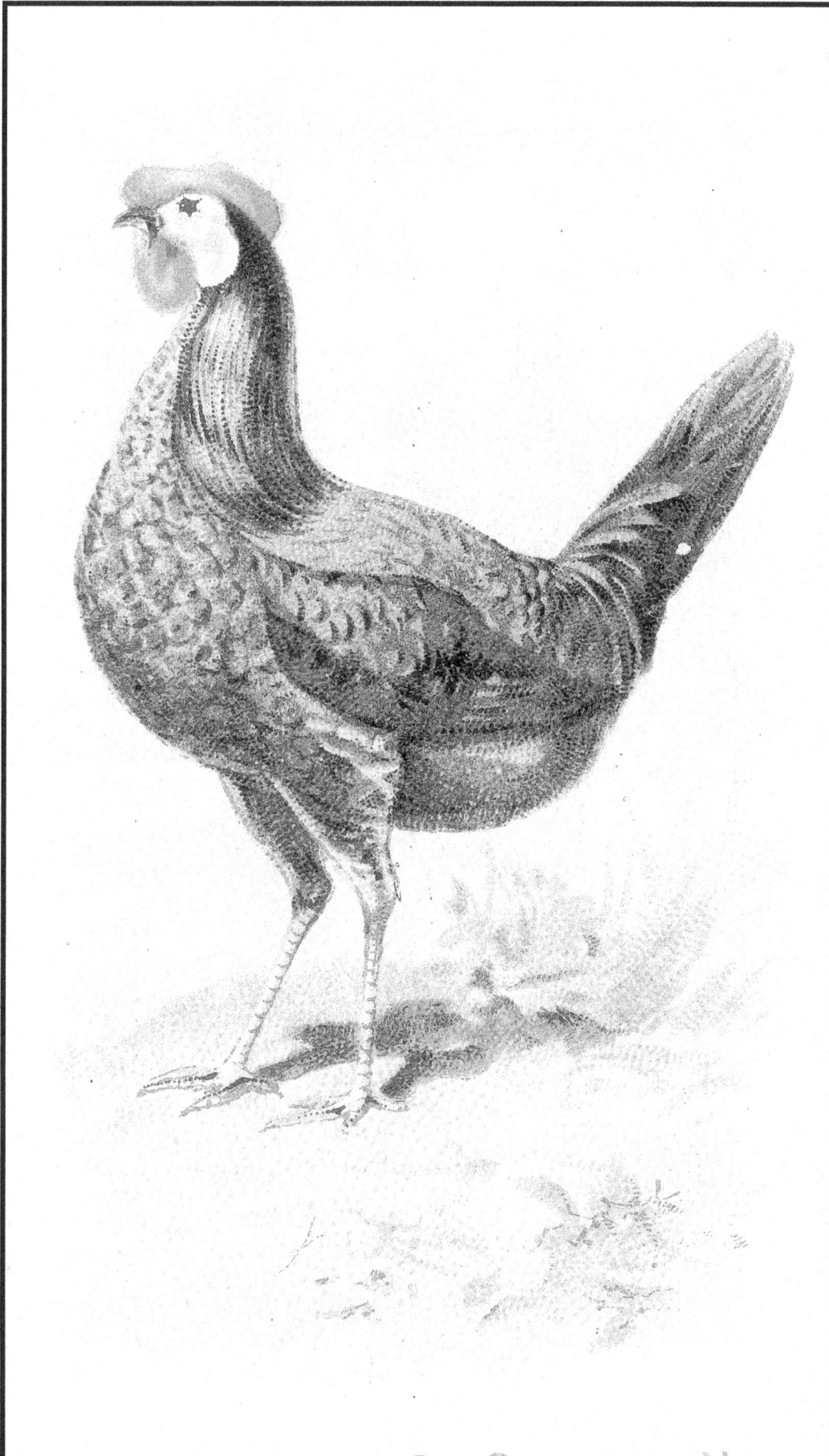

WHITE-FACED BL. SPANISH HEN.

WHEATEN GAME HEN.

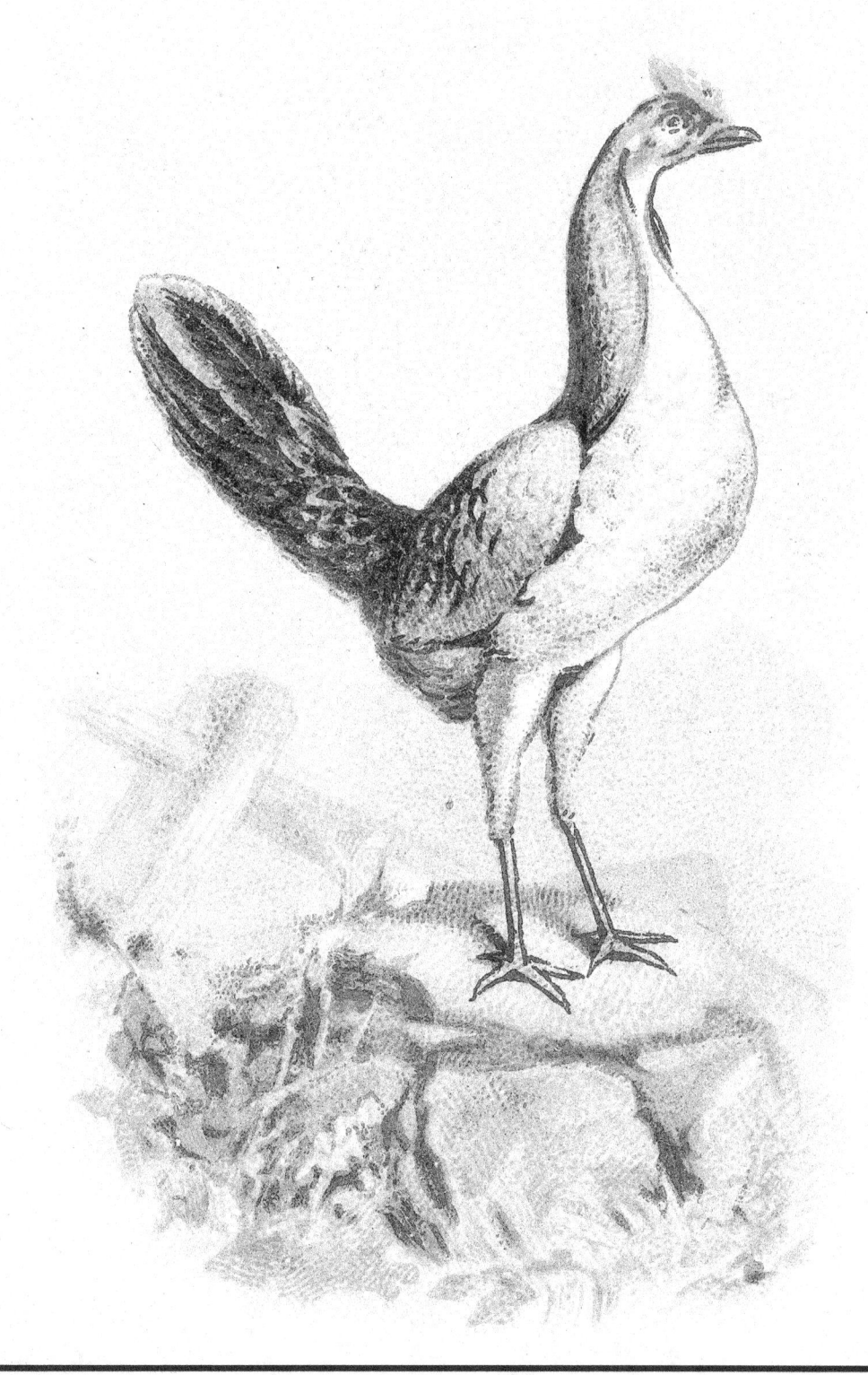

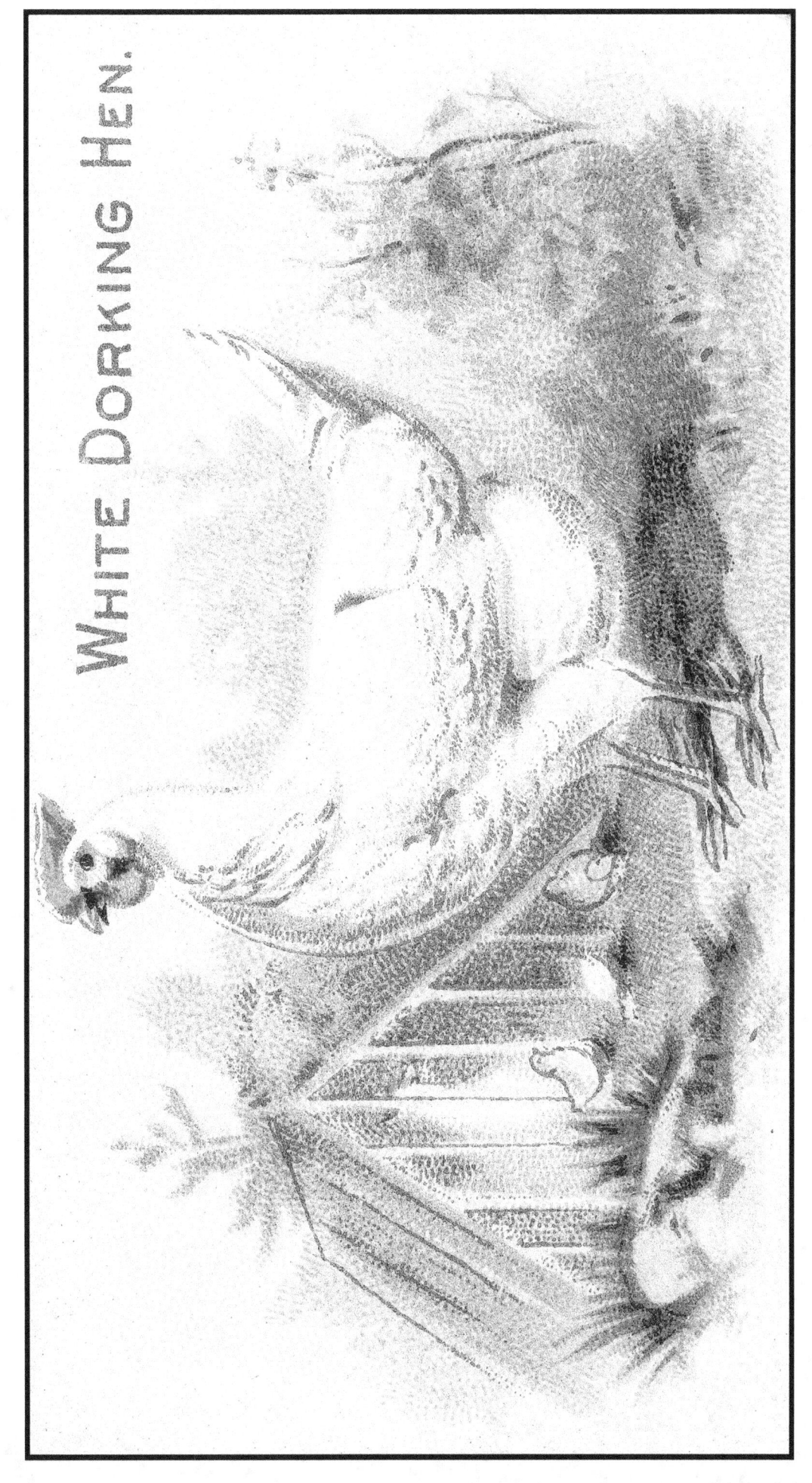

White Dorking Hen.

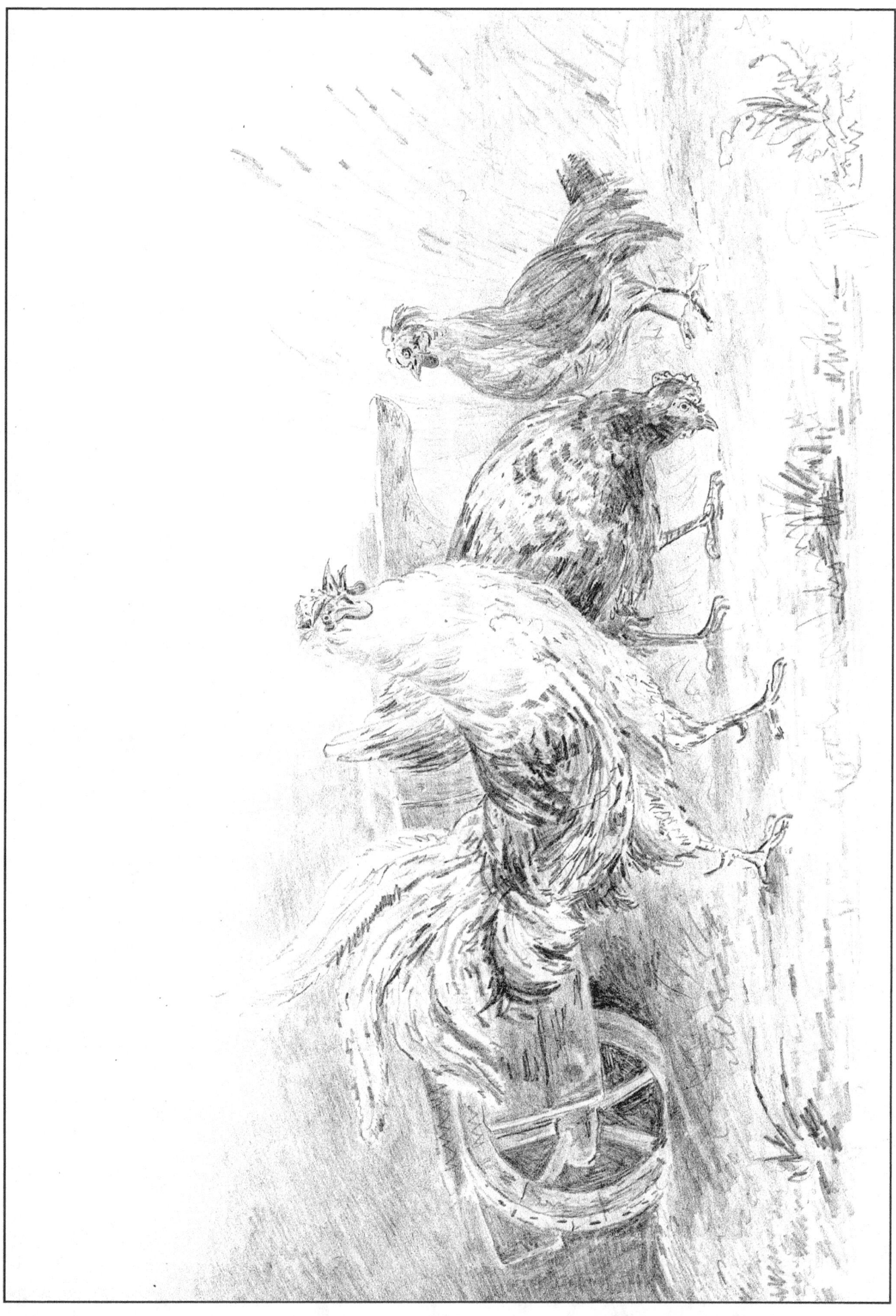

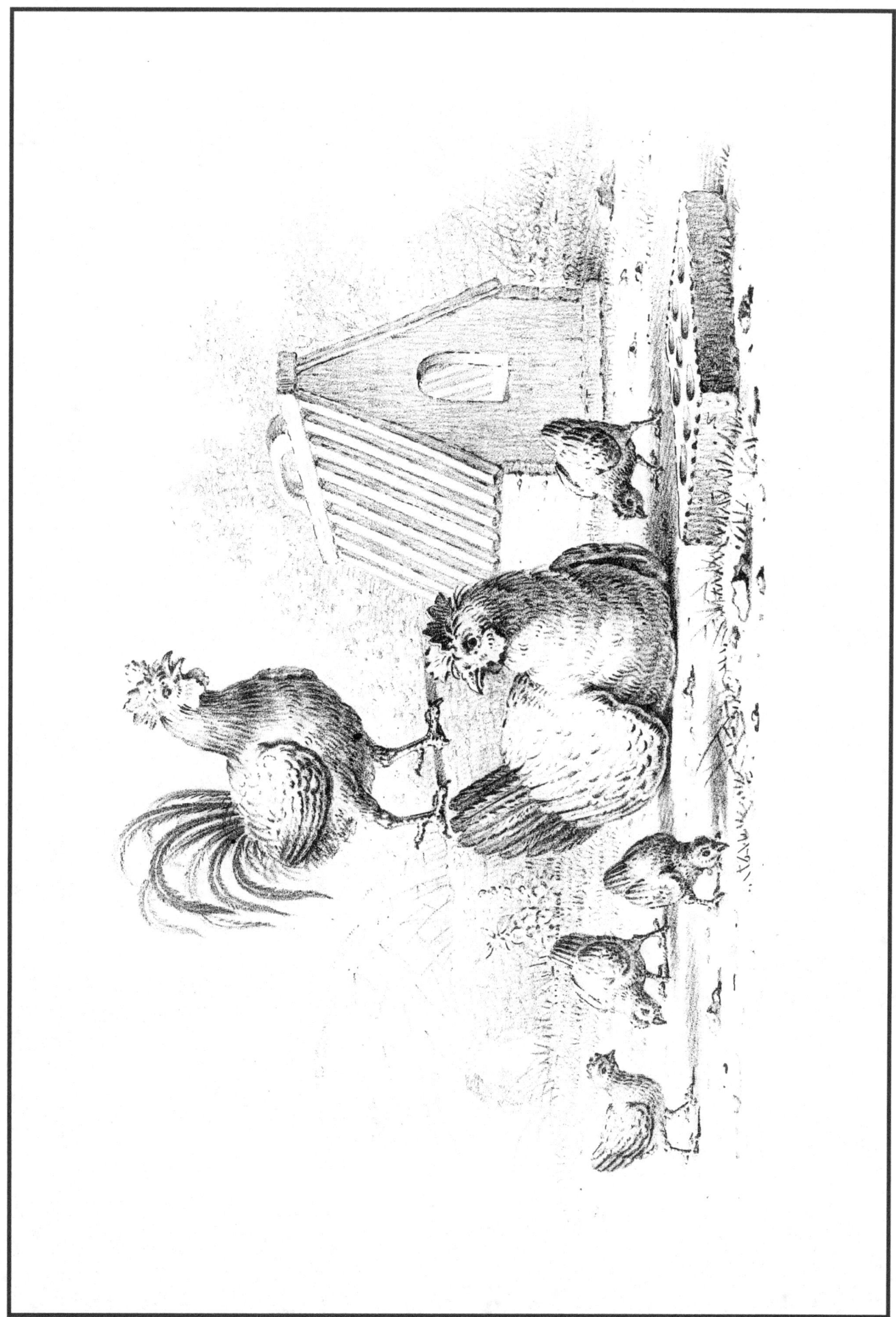

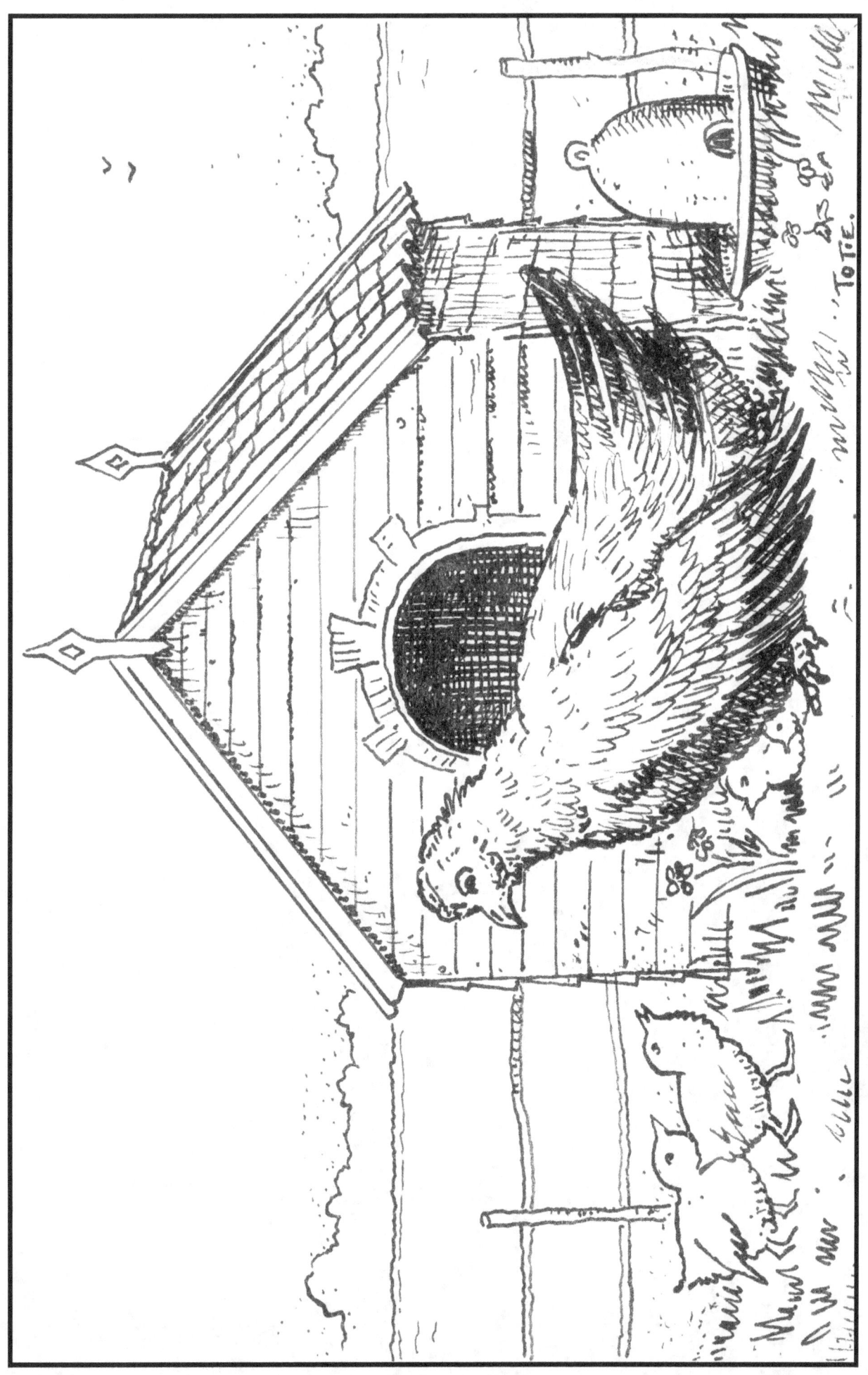

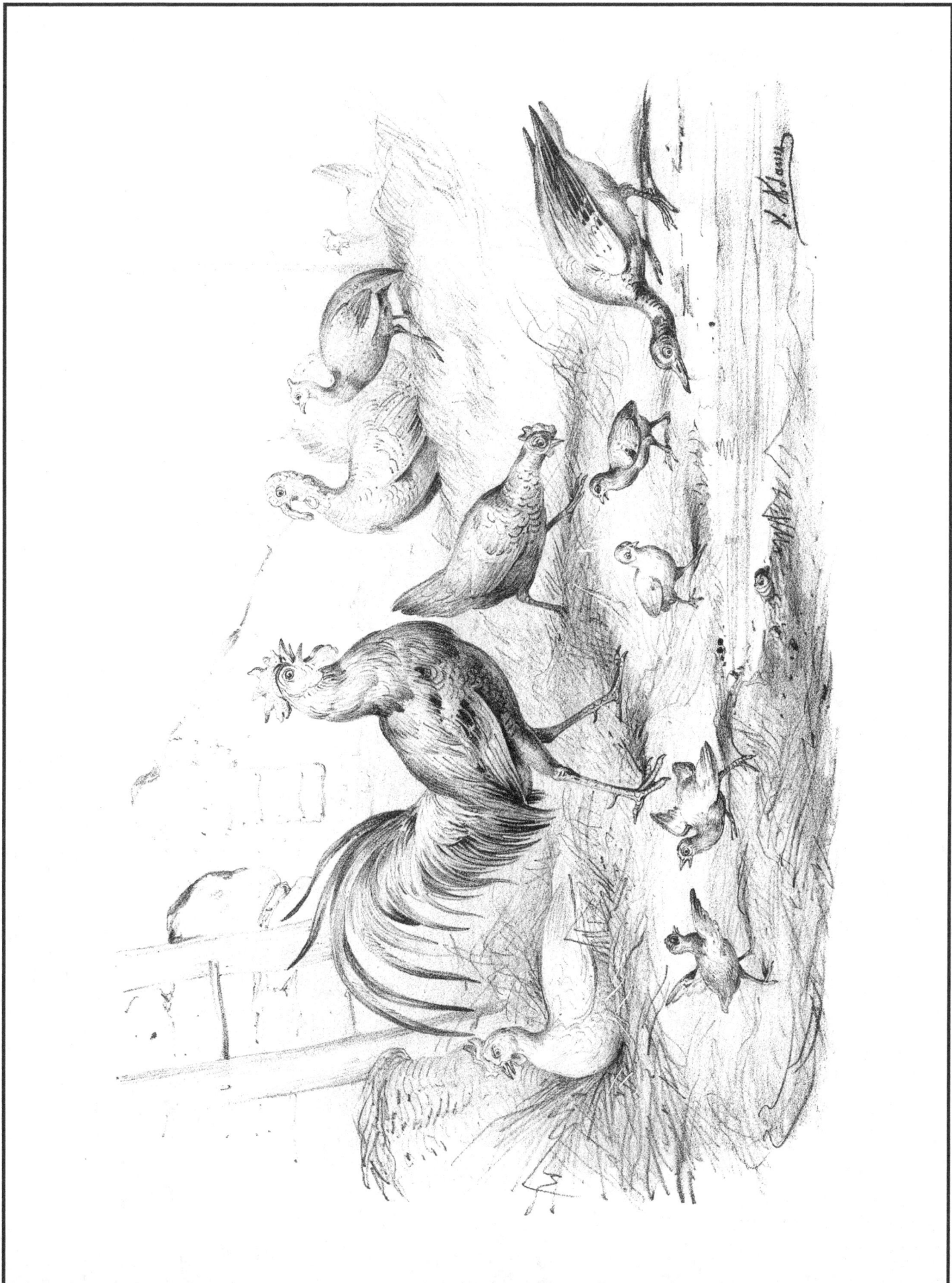

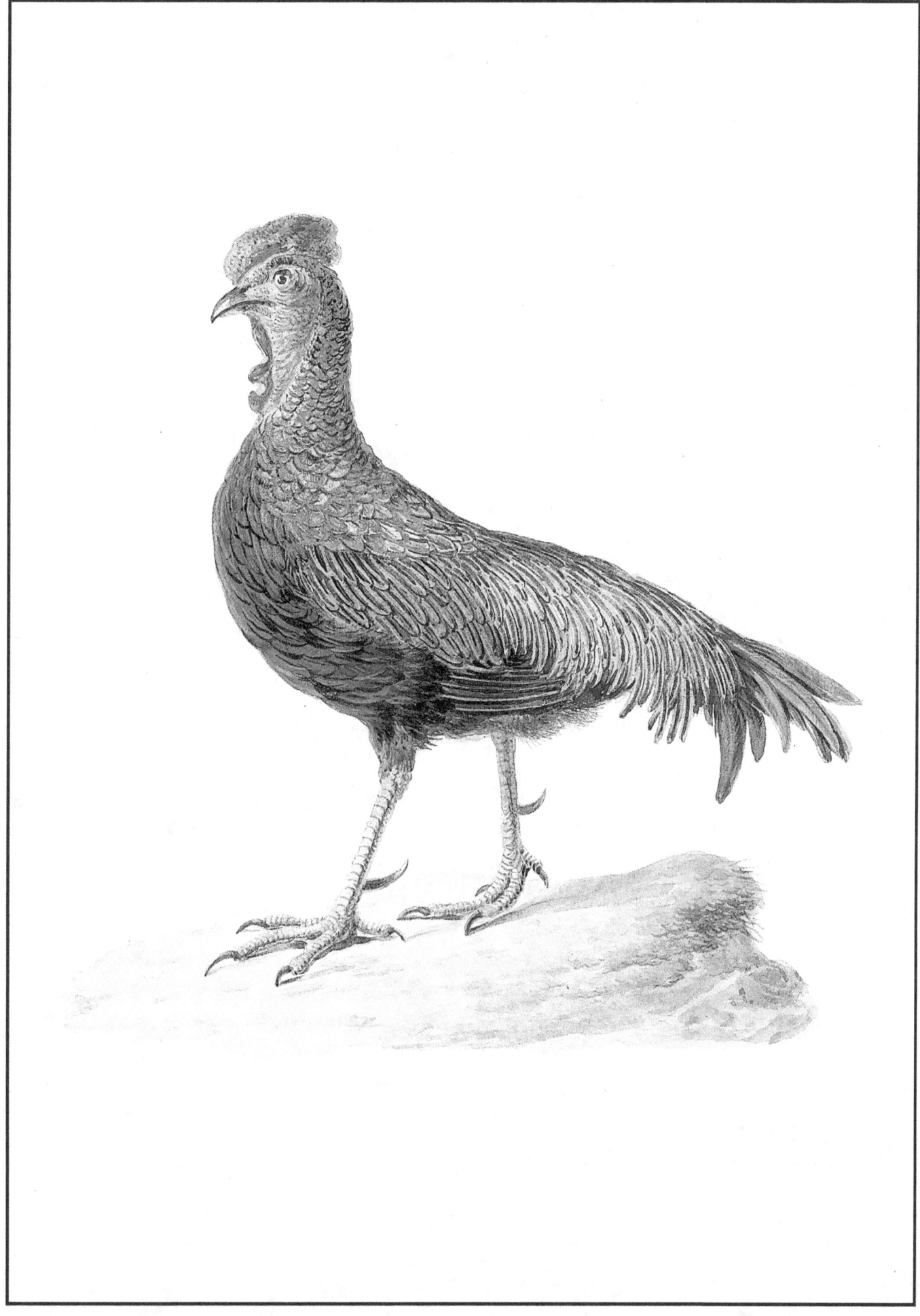

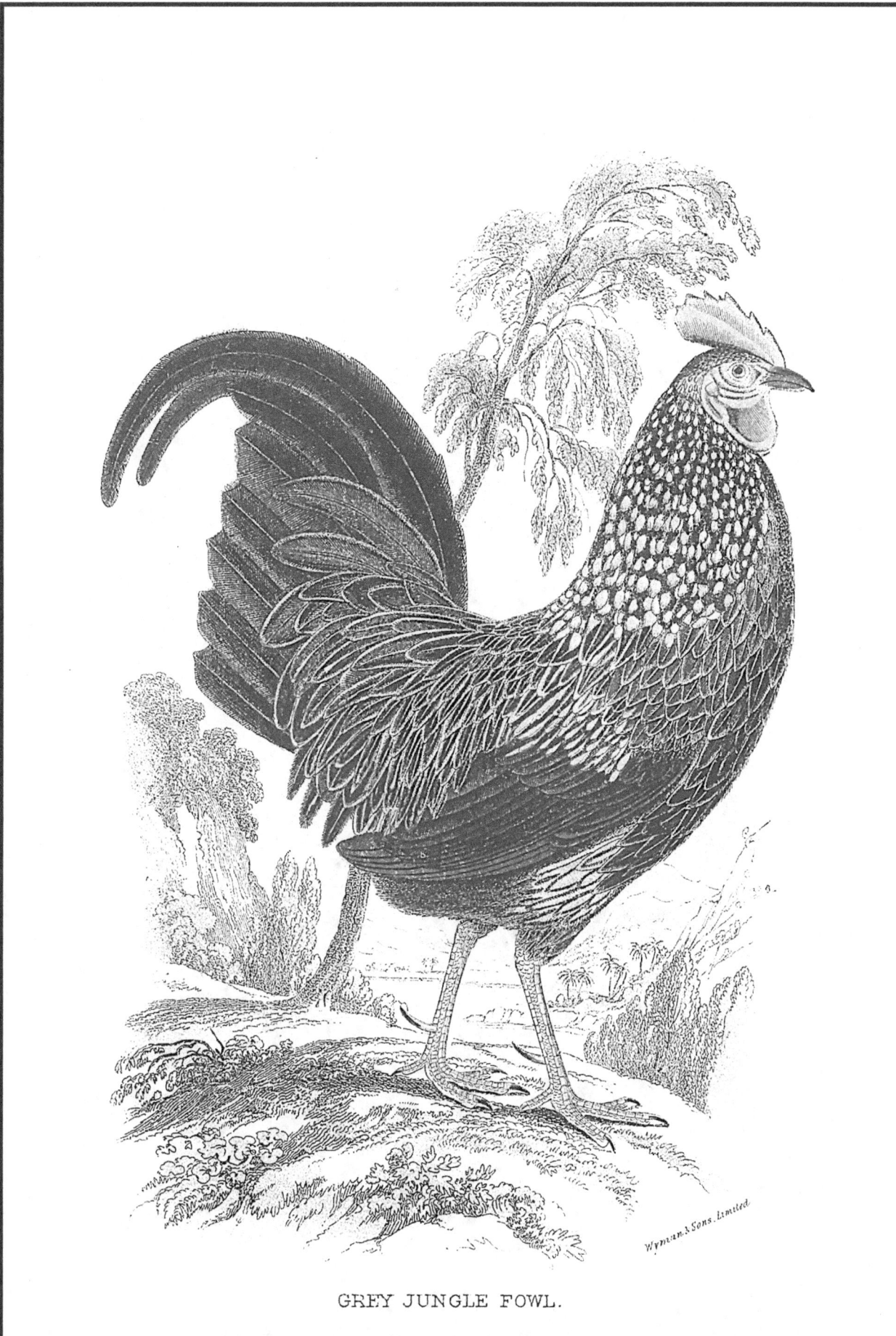

GREY JUNGLE FOWL.

www.ingramcontent.com/pod-product-compliance
Lightning Source LLC
Chambersburg PA
CBHW081520220526
45467CB00010B/2995